THE COMPLETE GUIDE TO THE MALTESE

Jordan Pogorzelski
and
Coral Drake

LP Media Inc. Publishing

For information address LP Media Inc. Publishing, 3178 253rd Ave. NW, Isanti, MN 55040

www.lpmedia.org

Publication Data

Jordan Pogorzelski and Coral Drake

The Complete Guide to the Maltese – First edition.

Summary: "Successfully raising a Maltese Dog from puppy to old age" – Provided by publisher.

ISBN: 978-1-954288-24-9

[1. Maltese – Non-Fiction] I. Title.

Design by Sorin Rădulescu

First paperback edition, 2021

TABLE OF CONTENTS

INTRODUCTION
Micah the Maltese

Being raised in a family that fostered dogs, I have been around breeds of all shapes, sizes, ages, and personalities for my entire life. Amongst all breeds, loyal little lap dogs have always caught my attention. Many small breeds have negative connotations surrounding them, particularly being associated as ankle biters, unintelligent, and prone to potty issues. Maltese put those connotations to rest with their calm temperament, wit, and trainability.

In September of 2016, my father unexpectedly passed away. I found myself in the market for a therapy dog several months after the ordeal. Thanks to my lifelong experience with dogs, I knew what I wanted in a small breed that was hypoallergenic. I'm normally a proponent of adopting rather than shopping, but our options were extremely limited by these criteria.

We searched for a reputable breeder in the area and visited their storefront with an open mind and open heart. My wife and I drove separately, so she beat me into the store. When I entered through the front door, I saw that my wife was already holding a precious little Maltese. We both immediately fell in love. We were initially window shopping but left with a signed contract, receipt, and new puppy in hand.

Micah spent the first several years of his life living with my mother, wife, and I in my hometown in Wisconsin. Aside from Micah, the household was a revolving door of foster dogs. Micah quickly established himself as the 'dog whisperer' by rehabilitating foster dogs that came from abusive homes. My mom's house was like a 24/7 doggie paradise for him.

In 2019, Micah, my wife, and I decided to make a change in our lives – we moved to Salt Lake City, Utah to enjoy all the recreational opportunities that Utah has to offer. Micah surprised us by morphing into an outdoors dog. He regularly stomps out four-mile hikes with ease and set a personal best of eight miles.

Nowadays, Micah is five years old and has settled into the apartment lifestyle in Utah nicely. He enjoys his peace and quiet at home during the day while his parents work. We spend our free time camping and hiking on the weekends. Micah proudly sports nicknames including Mister Lickers, Muffy, and Schnookies. He is kind, gentle, smart, and caring. We are proud to be parents of Micah.

Afterall, it's his world and we're just living in it.

Jordan Pogorzelski

Hiking with Micah

CHAPTER 1

Maltese History and Description

Malta

The islands of Malta, near Greece, have been populated since prehistoric times. Malta's history goes back to the beginning of civilization. Temples built in Malta are some of the oldest free-standing monuments in the world. They were built even before the Great Pyramids and Stonehenge.

The culture developed in Malta was unique and existed largely without outside influence until the Phoenicians settled in Malta around 750 BC. Part of this unique culture was the little white dog now known as the Maltese, which became popular throughout Rome and Europe. Once Malta was settled by the world-traveling Phoenicians, the Maltese dog found its way across the world.

Photo Courtesy of Barbara Shewmake Storybook Maltese

Photo Courtesy of Leona Lupulesku Leona's Maltese

Maltese travel the world

Aristocrats across the world, particularly ladies, were taken with this charming little dog. The 4th and 5th centuries BC Greeks were particularly fascinated by the geometric beauty of the Maltese. Aristotle refers to the dog as being perfectly proportioned despite its diminutive stature. The Greeks erected tombs in honor of their beloved Maltese.

Rome was also obsessed with the breed. Maltese are evident throughout Roman myths and fables. The dog stands as a symbol of loyalty throughout the stories. It is said that women did not consider themselves ready to go out if they did not have a Maltese peeking out of a sleeve or robe.

Ancient Egyptians built pyramids for their Maltese. There is a good chance that this breed was one of those worshipped by ancient Egyptians as a godly figure.

In the Bible, Paul recounts a story in the Acts of Apostles being shipwrecked on Malta. Paul healed the father of the island's Roman governor and was presented with a Maltese in gratitude.

During Europe's Dark Ages, the Chinese kept the Maltese breed alive. By the time Maltese were imported back to Europe, native Chinese toy breeds had created a more refined Maltese. This remarkable breed has maintained its standards throughout time. In 1877, it was exhibited at the first Westminster Dog Show, labeled as the Maltese Lion Dog.

Always a lapdog

Many toy breeds were originally bred for a job, such as pursuing rats or other small game. Other small breeds were bred down from larger dogs who previously had jobs, such as the King Charles Cavalier Spaniel or the Toy Poodle.

The Maltese, on the other hand, has never had any job other than being a loving companion. Throughout their long and esteemed history, they have been the dogs of royalty and the upper classes, kept not for function but for pleasure.

Thousands of years of breeding for temperament have resulted in one of the most delightful companions you are likely to find. These are confident, outgoing little dogs who seem to know no fear.

Maltese generally choose to be near their person, but they are aware of what is going on throughout their house. This makes them effective

Photo Courtesy of Michelle Lewis

watchdogs, although you can't rely on them to do anything to stop the intruder once they're inside except to charm them.

Micah is attached at my hip throughout the day but remains attentive to the outside world. When I'm sitting on the couch, he chooses to lay high up on the pillows behind my head. He chooses this high vantage point so that he can have a clear view out of the living room window. Once he sees someone walking by, he barks furiously unless I tell him otherwise. He barks a big bark, but in reality, he's too gentle to inflict any harm if he had the chance.

FUN FACT
American Maltese Association (AMA)

The American Maltese Association (AMA) was founded in 1961 as a combination of the Maltese Dog Club of America and Maltese Dog Fanciers of America. The AMA became an official member club of the American Kennel Club (AKC) on June 10, 1969, and is now the official parent club for the Maltese in America. As of 2019, there were over 250 members of the AMA.

Physical characteristics

Maltese are one of the most physically striking dogs of any breed or size. They have an aristocratic bearing with elegant movement and excellent balance.

Coat

Perhaps the first thing that stands out about a Maltese is its glorious coat. From the tip of the nose to the end of the tail, Maltese are covered with a long, silky mantle of white hair. The coat should always be pure white, although some staining around the eyes and mouth is to be expected.

Light tan or lemon in the ears is allowable but not desirable. Any pigment other than this is not acceptable by American Kennel Club (AKC) standards. The single coat tends not to shed and may be less prone to matting than other breeds since kinkiness, curliness, or wooly texture is undesirable.

Micah is always receiving compliments on his beautiful white coat but deals with some staining around his eyes and mouth. As aesthetically pleasing as the coat is to the eyes, it is equally pleasing to the touch. Unlike other breeds that have course fur, Maltese have fur that is as soft as feathers.

Size

Photo Courtesy of Kathleen Engelen

Maltese are very little dogs. They should always be under 7 lbs, with 4 to 6 lbs being preferable. The Maltese are perfectly proportioned, unlike small breed dogs who have shortened legs, such as the Dachshund or the Pekingese. Maltese have been prized for their ideal proportions throughout history, and perfect proportions are still very important for the breed today.

Micah is on the larger end of the spectrum. Although purebred, he weighs in at 10 lbs. According to his veterinarian, he isn't overweight by any means but is just simply on the larger side of the spectrum. It's important to check with your shelter or breeder to inquire about the size of your new puppy's parents. The size of the parents is a great indicator as to how large you should expect your dog to grow to.

Features

The Maltese have a rounded head with a cute "stop," or forehead, that helps to give the face its expressiveness. Droopy ears are low set and tend to be lost in the flow of hair when the dog is kept in full coat. When ears are kept clipped short, the dogs have a sweet, mobile, expressive nature.

I prefer to keep Micah's hair on the shorter end, which makes his features more prominent. The short hair prevents matting issues that are prevalent amongst Maltese's. It also gives him more of a teddy bear look than a traditional Maltese show dog look.

The eyes of a Maltese are very dark and round, and the whites should not be visible. Eyes are not set too far apart and tend to give the impression of looking forward. Black rims and long eyelashes add further drama to the beauty of a Maltese's expression. The tail is very distinct, as it tends to be carried over the back with a tip lying to one side.

Behavioral characteristics

"Maltese are carefree, happy dogs that are eager to please. They are happiest when they are with their person or people. They are one of the few toy breeds that enjoy well behaved children as well as all family members. They are very sensitive and make great companions for elderly and sick people."

KARAN ORSIN
Petite Pups

This gregarious little dog is playful, outgoing, and trusting. A Maltese is ready to befriend anyone but maintains a fierce loyalty to its own family. This is a dog who you can trust to be friendly towards your friends and defensive against your enemies.

Adaptable and outgoing

The Maltese started its existence with island life, but as the breed spread across the planet, the breed learned to live in all sorts of climates and situations. The outgoing, adaptable nature of the Maltese has made the breed well suited to change.

Maltese seem to look through rose-colored glasses at everything that happens in their world. They are not the least bit resistant to change, rather seeming to plunge with enthusiasm into every new experience. If you want a best friend who's ready to take on the world with you, the Maltese may be the dog for you.

The best example I can give of a Maltese's adaptability is Micah's travel enthusiasm. I frequently fly with Micah as a pet in-cabin. When traveling through a crowded, foreign airport, Micah isn't the least bit scared. He remains observant but calm. Once on the plane, Micah does not mind sitting in a closed travel bag and lays nicely underneath my seat for the duration of the flight. He sleeps soundly throughout the flight and never whimpers or whines.

Micah is also a great camping and hiking buddy. My fiancé and I live in Salt Lake City, Utah, and frequently camp in the Wasatch Mountains as well as the southern desert. Micah loves joining us on our trips and shows no signs of anxiety or discomfort. In fact, he seems to enjoy the change of scenery.

CHAPTER 2
Who Should Own a Maltese?

"A Maltese dog is a great choice for those in a small apartment or that don't get out much. They have a reputation for being 'couch potatoes'. They will enjoy an enthusiastic game of 'chase the ball' around the house or yard once or twice a day and then are quite happy to lounge and snooze the rest of the day, preferably in your lap. If you're looking for a hiking buddy, you may want to consider another breed."

BARBARA SHEWMAKE
Storybook Maltese

Photo Courtesy of Martha Burns

The adaptable, outgoing Maltese is a wonderful choice for most people. If you aren't sure what changes may happen in your life, a Maltese may be a good dog for you. This rough and tumble little pup is just as happy living on the top story of a skyscraper apartment building or with a pack of dogs on a ranch.

FUN FACT
What Were They Bred For?

Maltese dogs have a rich history dating back thousands of years. Ancient Greeks treasured this breed, going so far as to commemorate their dogs on pottery and with elaborate tombs. These small dogs were initially bred as watchdogs, companions, and status symbols for ancient aristocrats. The Maltese makes an excellent companion dog in modern times and can be ideal for sensitive groups due to their low shedding coat. Though they are energetic dogs, Maltese don't require excessive exercise and are usually content with a daily neighborhood walk to meet their needs.

Just be sure that everyone else in the family is respectful of your little Maltese's diminutive stature and delicate body, and he will be more than happy to get along with everybody. These are excellent boat dogs and a favorite of anyone who needs to travel for long periods, such as truckers or those who live in an RV.

I can also vouch that Maltese are great dogs for living in small apartments. Micah lives comfortably within my one-bedroom apartment. There is plenty of room within a one-bedroom apartment for a Maltese to stretch its legs and get adequate exercise while playing with toys.

Maltese can make good service dogs, as they're hypoallergenic, and their small size makes it easy to take them everywhere. Their outgoing personality means they won't mind sticking with you through all of your day's adventures. Whether you want a loving companion to come home to at the end of a long day or a constant friend for everything you do, the Maltese is a good choice.

Micah used to travel with us as an Emotional Support Animal, which is similar to a service animal. My fiancé obtained a written letter from her doctor that qualified Micah as an Emotional Support Animal. He does a great job of helping my fiancé manage her in-flight anxiety. Unfortunately, many airlines no longer accept Emotional Support Animal waivers.

That said, there are some important considerations when deciding whether a Maltese is right for you. Here are some things to keep in mind about this amazing breed.

Delicate

Be aware that this is not just a small dog but an extremely small dog. The difference between five pounds and ten pounds can be dramatic. Keep in mind that a Maltese puppy is especially delicate for the first year. A puppy may weigh only a couple of pounds and be severely injured by a drop of only a foot or so. Due to this, Maltese are not best for small children, unruly households, or big dog siblings.

Because Maltese are so fearless and often seem to be lacking in an instinct for self-preservation, they are likely to get themselves into a situation where they might get injured in the wrong household. As such, Maltese are wonderful dogs for older children who know how to be respectful and will not accidentally drop them. They do well with dogs of all sizes, provided the other dogs are careful not to step on them or knock into them.

As I hike with my dog, I notice him attempting to scale large rocks and other obstacles that may result in an injury. He is completely fearless and confident in his abilities. As athletic as he is, I help him scale these sketchy obstacles because I don't want to see him injured.

Photo Courtesy of Gabriele Puplauskaite

His paw pads are similarly delicate. If you plan on taking your Maltese on long walks or hikes, then you must be mindful of its paw pads. The thin paw pads aren't designed for high-mileage trips and are easily irritated. When I go on long hikes, I bring along a carrying backpack for him and put him in it if I notice his paws are becoming irritated.

Speak their mind

Your Maltese will be sure to let you know if someone is arriving at your house. Without proper training, he may also alert you to the goings-on throughout the neighborhood, leading to continuous yapping. This tends to be a vocal breed, especially when it comes to alerting you. Because Maltese can be a bit on the headstrong side, they need firm leadership in order to learn when it is appropriate to alert and when they should stay quiet. If you're looking for an exceptionally quiet breed, this isn't it.

Micah is quite vocal when he sees someone walking their dog outside of our window. He is similarly vocal when he wants to be let inside after a potty break. When it comes to food, Micah was quite the beggar and would often whine. It took quite a bit of training to get him to stop vocally begging for food.

Smart and stubborn

"Maltese can be considered clingy. Depending on the dog this can be either mild or extreme. If they are extremely clingy it can evolve into separation anxiety, which is not desired. Getting items that stimulate their mind or toys to keep them busy when they have to be left alone will help to curb these tendencies."

SHARON PEARSON
Foxstone Maltese

The Maltese are intelligent and highly trainable. They love learning tricks and are emotionally attuned to their owner, making them an excellent pick for service dog work as well as anyone who wants a very loyal pet. That said, Maltese do not live to serve you. Think of them more as dogs who live to be your friends.

Your Maltese wants to make you happy but has a mind of its own. He will bend the rules or straight up disobey if he thinks he can get away with it. A Maltese is much too sensitive for any kind of negative training, so it is essential that you practice firm and consistent training throughout his life if you don't want to end up with a dog who does what he wants instead of what you want.

Positive reinforcement is the best way to get through to your Maltese. Try rewarding your dog for its good behavior rather than scolding your dog for its bad behavior. If you too viciously scold your Maltese, then he may hold a grudge against you that can last several days. They don't forget being mistreated.

Athletic and demand interaction

Photo Courtesy of Irina Korovyakovskaya

Maltese don't need much exercise, and they tend to be laid back, especially compared to many terrier breeds, but they do demand a certain level of physical exercise and mental stimulation. If you don't give your Maltese the exercise and training that he craves, he will find other ways to occupy himself.

With Maltese, this often means vocalizing, either by barking about whatever is going on around your house or barking directly at you for engagement. This is a dog who is happy to hang out with you and watch TV all night, but you better also be ready for a game of fetch, a good walk, or a round of trick training before you settle down to relax.

I can tell when my dog is bored when he starts getting into things that he shouldn't. For example, if I don't play with him enough throughout the day, then he will start moving shoes around the house. If he's really bored, he will let me know by chewing through a pair of shoes. To mitigate his boredom, I take Micah on daily walks and play with him throughout the day.

Must be groomed regularly

Photo Courtesy of Peggy Summitt

The low shedding and largely hypoallergenic coat of a Maltese is a major plus for most people. The silky texture of the coat tends not to mat as easily as in some other breeds, but the coat must still be brushed at least once or twice a day in order to prevent tangling and matting. Most owners who are not showing their Maltese choose to keep them in a short clip, such as the puppy cut.

Even a short coat must be brushed out every couple of days in order to avoid mats forming against the skin. The large, luminous eyes of the Maltese often leak, resulting in tear staining, which can irritate your dog's skin unless the eye area is cleaned regularly. Add to this the regular chores of nail trimming and ear cleaning, and you have a fairly significant grooming task on your hands regularly.

Since a Maltese dog is small, grooming will not take as long as it would for a larger dog of a similar coat, but it is still significant. If you don't think you are up for lots of brushing and don't want to clip your dog yourself or pay for a groomer, a short-coated dog, or a dog with a rough coat that can be stripped instead of cut, may be a better option for you.

I personally keep Micah's hair short. The puppy cut prevents my dog's hair from matting, which is a serious problem. I cannot stress enough the importance of regularly brushing your Maltese dog's coat. This not only keeps it soft but also prevents matting. It's incredibly difficult to brush out thick mats, so it's important to be proactive in preventing them.

Micah develops mats most commonly on his ears and armpits. I can tell that they cause him discomfort. I can tell when he has a mat because he frequently scratches and attempts to untangle them himself. In severe scenarios, his nails have gotten caught in his mats while scratching, which causes him pain.

As far as his eyes go, Micah deals with significant tear staining. Although it doesn't appear to cause him any discomfort, it's important to regularly clean the eyes of your Maltese to prevent staining.

To prevent staining, it is recommended that you feed your dog out of ceramic dishes rather than metallic dishes. If you have high iron content in your water or if your water has a high hardness level, then it is more likely that you will deal with staining. Try giving your dog filtered water instead of water straight out of the tap in this situation. There are also products available on the market that can prevent staining.

Long-lived and generally healthy

Maltese tend to be a healthy breed. This perfectly proportioned little dog doesn't suffer from the back issues that short-legged breeds do and doesn't have a brachycephalic (short) nose, excessive wrinkles, or anything else that may result in physical issues.

Maltese can suffer from luxating patella like most toy breeds, and it is important to keep track of your Maltese's heart health, but in general, you can expect your Maltese to live well over a decade and generally into its teens.

Generally critter-friendly

In general, Maltese are good-natured and friendly with everyone they meet, both animal and human. They get on well with other dogs and easily form friendly relationships with new dogs. Typically Maltese don't care whether other dogs are much bigger than them, as long as the other dogs are respectful of their small size.

Maltese are confident and friendly enough to form good relationships with other household pets like cats, rabbits, and larger birds. That said, some large cats may play too rough or see a Maltese as a prey object.

While Maltese have never been used expressly for the hunting of small animals, some may still have a prey drive, especially with very small creatures like rats, mice, and tiny birds. For the best luck with such animals, introduce your Maltese early and always supervise interactions.

I foster dogs and frequently have two to three dogs in my house at all times. Micah is warm and welcoming to foster dogs of all shapes, sizes, and ages. He is never gotten into a physical altercation with another dog. Micah also gets along well with our pet guinea pig.

Great travel companions

Maltese are first-class traveling companions. These diminutive dogs can fit into your purse or a carrier with ease. When trained to travel, they are generally very quiet and tolerant, so most people won't even notice that you have a dog. Maltese can be trained to use litter boxes or can also be paper trained, in addition to going outdoors. They are good watchdogs over your boat or vehicle and tend to thrive on the routine of relaxation and excitement that is characteristic of traveling.

When Micah travels with us, it's important that we take him to the bathroom prior to arriving at the airport. Many airlines recommend not feeding or giving water to your dog for up to four hours before a flight. This gives your dog time to fully clear its bowels. Many airports have pet relief areas, although they are often horribly kept. Micah refuses to use pet relief areas in airports.

CHAPTER 3
Buy or Adopt?

It can be very hard to decide whether you want to buy your new Maltese from a responsible breeder or adopt a homeless Maltese in need. You are unlikely to find a purebred Maltese puppy who needs to be rescued, except in the rare case of a puppy mill or backyard breeding operation that is broken up by authorities. You may, however, find Maltese mix puppies available for adoption from a rescue. Here are some advantages of buying or adopting.

Buy	Adopt
Predictable. By choosing an AKC registered breeder, you know exactly what you are getting, both in health and temperament, and can control what your pup experiences.	**Affordable.** Adoption prices are generally in the hundreds rather than the thousands.
Time. By buying a puppy, you have the best chance of having a full 12 to 15 years to spend with your dog.	**Save a life.** A homeless dog really needs you, and a dog who has suffered in their life may appreciate you more than a puppy who has always had everything.
Availability. Maltese puppies are generally available from quality breeders several times a year, while you may have a hard time finding a rescue.	**Less commitment.** Adopt an older dog or foster a dog if you can't commit 15 years.

Choosing a breeder

The Maltese is a relatively popular breed, and quality breeders are not in short supply. Consult The American Maltese Association (http://www.americanmaltese.org/) in order to find an AKC registered breeder in your area. Buying from an AKC breeder means that you know your dog's bloodline is true to the traits desirable in the Maltese. It does not, however, necessarily mean that the breeder is raising the best puppies for you to choose from. Here are a few things to look for in the AKC registered breeder that you decide to purchase from.

QUESTIONS TO ASK THE BREEDER

- Have the parents been screened for cardiac and patella problems?
- Have there ever been incidences of cardiac or patella problems in any dogs in the line?
- Can we meet the parents?
- Are all dogs up-to-date on vaccinations?
- Do you have restrictions on whether we can breed the dog that we get from you?

Photo Courtesy of Barbara Shewmake Storybook Maltese

About breeder contracts

Breeder contracts clarify exactly which dog you are buying and its lineage, as well as your information as the buyer. They also include all of the expectations that the breeder has in regard to how you care for your dog. You can expect to see registration numbers and, of course, the price for the puppy that you are buying. Here are some other things that you may see in a breeder contract.

SHOW VERSUS PET

Some puppies have show potential, which means that they may grow up to be competitive in the show ring. Sometimes breeders specify that they want to see a puppy at a certain age and decide whether they want to take it from you temporarily to show it at dog shows and potentially breed it.

The contract will also clarify what will happen if it is decided that the dog should be bred. If a dog does not have show potential, the breeder contract may require that the dog be spayed or neutered and will probably require that the dog not be bred.

RETURN TO BREEDER

If you decide to rehome the dog at any point, responsible breeders will want to know about it. They may request that the dog be returned to them so that they can make decisions about rehoming, or they may just want to know where the dog goes when it is returned.

HEALTH GUARANTEES

Health guarantees are put into the breeder contract to protect the buyer against genetic defects that the dog may have, often up to a particular age. They may also cover particular ailments like heart problems or hip dysplasia. The health concerns that are covered will vary by breed and breeder.

NAMING CONVENTIONS

Your breeder will probably want the puppies to be registered with AKC. Some breeders ask that you do the registration while others take care of it themselves. Regardless of who registers the puppy, it will need a longer registered name along with a short call name. Sometimes breeders will ask that the kennel name is part of the puppy's registered name, or they may want the name to start with a particular letter or have a theme.

Photo Courtesy of Karen Crawford

Raised in the home

When breeding very large, active breeds such as pointers, shepherds, etc., it is understandable for even responsible breeders to raise dogs in a kennel. Serious breeders generally have at least five or six and easily up to a dozen or more dogs, and keeping so many large breed dogs in the home is unreasonable for many people.

However, when you are considering a tiny breed like the Maltese, whose entire role in life is to be an excellent companion, you want to choose a breeder who keeps breeding dogs in their home and raises puppies with their family. Puppies become aware of the world as soon as they are born, so you want puppies that have been exposed to regular home life from the beginning.

If a breeder keeps Maltese litters outdoors in unsanitary conditions and in cages much too small, then that is a strong indicator of a puppy mill. If you believe that your breeder is running a puppy mill, then please be sure to report it to the proper authority.

Performs required and additional health screens

The National Maltese Club recommends that Maltese be screened for heart health with a cardiac exam and receive an evaluation to be sure that breeding dogs are free of symptomatic luxating patella. However, there are other more potential problems in the Maltese breed that a very responsible breeder should be screening for. This includes a bile test for congenital liver issues such as liver shunt and microvascular dysplasia. Although most dogs live their entire lives asymptomatically, even if they do suffer from these diseases, you want to find a breeder who is working towards eliminating that in their puppies.

Encephalitis is a condition that has been found in Maltese as well as other toy breeds. It is thought that this form of meningitis is an autoimmune response in which the body attacks itself, resulting in inflammation in the central nervous system, especially the brain. A test does not yet exist to determine whether puppies may come down with the disease, but your breeder should be upfront about whether any Maltese in their breeding lines has exhibited neurologic symptoms in the past.

Dental maintenance is important for all toy breeds. Your breeder should have regular dental checks performed on all of their breeding dogs, and even their older dogs should still have teeth in reasonably good condition.

I take Micah in for annual health screenings and make sure that I stay up to date with vaccinations. Annual health screenings also include a stool sample to check for parasites. It's important to establish a relationship with a veterinarian as soon as you adopt or purchase your new Maltese.

Asks you lots of questions

Choosing a breeder isn't just about you making the decision and making the purchase. A responsible breeder cares where their puppies end up. The breeder that you are considering should ask you questions about why you are choosing a Maltese puppy, what your lifestyle is like, and how you intend to take care of your dog. They may insist that you have your dog spayed or neutered or ask that you not spay or neuter in order that they may have breeding rights later on. Beware of breeders who don't care whether you spay, neuter, or breed your puppy or who don't have any questions to ask you.

Most breeders will require you to fill out a waiver that describes your living conditions. The waiver oftentimes includes questions about the style of your home (apartment, condo, house, etc.), the size of your home, your work schedule, and more. A responsible breeder will want to make sure that your home and lifestyle are good fits for one of their dogs.

The rescue shelter that I volunteer at goes as far as requiring home visits. The rescue shelter sends volunteers to applicants' homes to inspect. The inspector decides if the home is suitable for a rescue dog or not. The shelter also inquires about past pets, particularly if you have ever had to put down a pet in the past. The shelter does not want to adopt dogs out to owners who have prematurely put down their other pets.

Rescuing a Maltese

"If adopting from a rescue: try to find out the past history of the dog, this can be helpful in getting to know them and what you can expect. To get an idea of potential health issues, check the dog's teeth: Bad teeth can cause horrible health problems. Finally, be prepared to have lots of patience. Many rescues have abuse or neglect issues and it may take a long time for them to develop trust with you."

SHASTA GRIMES
Desert Hobby Ranch

It may be hard to imagine how anything as adorable, charming, and adoptable as a Maltese could find itself without a home. Unfortunately, Maltese are too often seen as status symbols which are bought for their beautiful coats but never taken care of or loved as a dog should be.

Maltese are frequent victims of puppy mills and backyard breeding since they are small enough to house and breed many of them in a relatively small space and can command a high price tag. Maltese are popular for cross-breeding with poodles as well, creating the popular mixed breed "designer dog," the Maltipoo.

Dogs that are useful for creating mixes, as well as purebreds, are especially desirable for breeding programs that are only for profit since there are more options with which dogs you can breed together and produce sellable puppies.

Luckily, the Maltese have a well-organized rescue on their side. The American Maltese Association Rescue (www.americanmalteserescue.org) is affiliated with the American Maltese Association, so they have a fair amount of resources and organization to help them do their job of getting homeless Maltese dogs to loving homes. You can also find Maltese available locally on sites like Adoptapet.com and Petfinder.com.

Picking your puppy

You've found the perfect breeder or rescue shelter, put down your deposit, and anxiously awaited the due date. Now it is time for you to go pick up your brand new Maltese puppy. Sometimes breeders will decide for you which Maltese puppy is the best for your needs. Other times you may only have one or two puppies in the litter to choose from after everybody else takes their pick.

If you put your deposit in early, you may have the entire litter to choose from. Well-bred Maltese are unlikely to deviate far from the breed standard either in appearance or personality, but there still can be a lot of variety between dogs in the litter. Here are a few things to keep in mind when choosing a Maltese from the litter:

Pick a puppy that matches your personality

You may be surprised by how much of a puppy's personality you can see even when the puppies are available for you to pick up at 10 or 12 weeks. You can also talk to the breeder about what kind of personality each puppy is showing. While dogs will continue to change a lot as they mature, some personality traits tend to come out early and persist throughout life.

Puppies who are bold, fearless, and adventurous often grow into confident, outgoing dogs. While you may assume that the puppy who jumps on you first is the one you want, if you have a more reserved or sensitive personality and want a Maltese that really shows the ability to connect with its human, it may be better to choose a quieter individual. Puppies who don't mind being beaten up by their littermates are likely to be less bold and adventurous and may be more placid and sensitive house pets.

It's important to spend as much time at the breeders or rescue as need be. Take your time in making this important decision. Make sure to interact with each and every puppy in the litter separately. Some dog's personalities differ depending on if they are in a group setting or a one-on-one setting.

Micah was the quiet, gentle dog within a large litter. The breeder told us that he was bullied by his siblings and was likely to be reserved and passive throughout his life. Once we separated Micah from his abusive siblings and brought him home with us, his personality took a turn. He grew into a highly confident and energetic dog but still has a gentle soul.

Do you want a highly responsive dog or a dog who can entertain itself?

When asked the question of whether they want a responsive dog, many people assume that they do. Of course, you want a dog who will respond to commands most of the time and who is human-focused... don't you? If you want to spend all of your time with your Maltese and teach him tricks or compete in sports like agility, then a highly responsive dog who is keyed into you is certainly what you are looking for. For a good working dog who will be responsive to you even through long tasks, look for the puppy who persists in trying to accomplish its goals and who is focused on you.

If you would rather have more of a roommate of a dog who will be happy to cuddle and hang out a lot of the time but who can entertain himself, then look for a puppy who is happy to take his toy to the corner and play alone. Such puppies may also be less likely to suffer separation anxiety as adults when you leave them alone and may be generally more easy-going.

Are you interested in show or breeding?

If you are choosing a Maltese simply to be your family's next pet, you may not care how closely it conforms to the breed standard physically, as long as the puppy is happy and healthy. If, on the other hand, you are in love with this gorgeous breed and want this to be your first foray into showing or breeding Maltese, then your decision becomes much more challenging.

Many breeders choose to keep the dogs with the best show quality for their own breeding lines or give such dogs to close friends, but if you can get your hands on a puppy that has show-quality, then you have more than a pet. A dog who has show and breeding potential is an investment, both for you, as you hope to someday make income from the stud fee or puppies, and an investment into the breed.

Becoming a breeder is a serious endeavor, and if you love the breed, then it is essential that you breed only the highest-quality dogs with the best possible health. Get ready to pay a much higher premium for a puppy who has show quality, and prepare yourself for disappointment. Many puppies who have beautiful conformation as puppies grow into dogs who do not do well in shows, either because their personality does not make them excel in this area or because they end up not conforming to breed standards once they're fully grown. Make sure that you will still love the puppy that you take home, regardless of whether he is show quality or not.

Deciding on an adult dog

If you have made the decision to rescue or purchase an adult dog, then you may be a little bit more apprehensive about the process of choosing your new pet. It's hard to go wrong choosing from a litter of adorable

Photo Courtesy of Toni Herhold

puppies, but adult dogs may come with baggage or medical issues that can affect your life together.

If your primary goal is to save the life of a Maltese who has found itself without a home, then you may want to save a dog regardless of potential issues. If, on the other hand, you want to get the best family pet that you can and are worried about potential issues, then here are some tips for choosing an adult dog who will be a perfect fit for your family with as few risks as possible.

Foster first

The absolute best way to get to know a dog before you make the commitment to ownership is fostering. Fostering allows you to keep the dog in your home for a time so that you can make sure that it is a good match for you, your family, and your lifestyle. If you have children, other pets, or anything that causes you to have a particular question about your new Maltese, then fostering first is even more useful.

Unfortunately, Maltese are usually highly adoptable, and you may not be able to find a rescue who is willing to allow you to foster before making a commitment to adopt. At the very least, inquire about medical issues that may come up in the first week or a policy that permits a refund within the first week or so if things don't work out.

I was raised in a family that fostered dogs. I can attest to the fact that this is the best way to get to know a foster dog before adopting it. My brother, my sister, and my mom have all adopted dogs that were first introduced to us as fosters.

Adopt a dog with a known history

While you cannot expect to learn everything from a dog's previous family or long-term foster family and there is always the potential for things to be hidden from you, choosing a dog with a known history that comes from a family that you can talk to makes it much more likely that you will be able to know your dog's personality and characteristics before you bring him home.

Breeders often retire their breeding dogs to family homes when the dogs are too old to breed or when some kind of medical issue, even very minor, arises. Breeders often need to have multiple dogs in their program in order to create the best possible lines, but it can become challenging to keep all of those dogs happy and healthy in the home, especially as dogs get older

FUN FACT
Millionaire Maltese

When billionaire businesswoman Leona Helmsley died, her Maltese, Trouble, inherited $12 million. This amount was reduced to $2 million, however, when a judge ruled that $12 million exceeded the amount necessary for the care of the dog and said that Ms. Helmsley was of unsound mind when the will was made. Trouble passed away on December 13, 2010. The money remaining in Trouble's trust at the time of her death has reverted to a trust for charitable purposes.

and live for potentially up to 10 years or more after they have retired from breeding.

Therefore, breeders may rehome dogs into a family home. This can be an awesome way to get an adult dog who has already had a good life, never faced abuse or neglect, and has excellent breeding. If you are interested in adopting an adult Maltese, then talk to breeders in your area about adopting one of their old breeding dogs.

Focus on what you need in a dog

You may have a very complete picture of what you want in your new Maltese dog. After all, you have chosen the Maltese breed for a reason, and there are certain characteristics of this breed that you expect to have in your dog. That said, it may be challenging to find an individual dog with all of the characteristics that you are looking for.

Prioritize what really matters to you in the dog that you choose. Perhaps you would like a dog-friendly dog, but in reality, you don't have any other dogs or go places with dogs often, so maybe that characteristic really isn't that important.

On the other hand, a characteristic like a dog who is cuddly and affectionate with you may be absolutely essential. Make sure that you know what you really need in a dog, and don't rule dogs out because of characteristics that don't really matter that much to you anyway.

Maltese mixes

As you are looking for a Maltese to adopt, especially if you are looking for older dogs in need of rescue, then you are likely to stumble upon several mixed breed dogs with Maltese in them. Breeders may mix Maltese with other white dogs that tend to have hair, such as the Bichon or the Poodle.

This results in a larger dog and an unpredictable coat. Although the coat will be hair rather than fur, it may be curly or cottony, rather than silky and straight like a Maltese, which may make matting more likely. Depending on what the mix is, Maltese mixes have different personalities as well.

Maltese mixed with outgoing dogs like the Bichon Frise or a spaniel are likely to be very outgoing and happy since the Maltese also tends to be an outgoing, happy dog. If, on the other hand, the Maltese dog is mixed with a more sensitive dog like a Poodle, then the mix may end up being more reserved and sensitive than the average happy-go-lucky Maltese.

Maltese mixed with terriers such as a schnauzer may show a much more confident personality with higher prey drive than what you would expect from a Maltese. If you are considering a Maltese mix, then it is important to research the other breeds that go into the mix so that you can have a better idea of what the dog will end up being like. Keep in mind that just because a mixed breed dog looks more like one breed or the other doesn't mean that their personality will follow their appearance.

CHAPTER 4

Getting to Know Your Adult Maltese

If you have made the decision to adopt an adult dog, especially if you don't know much about the dog's past or history, you will have to take some time to get to know your dog. Moving from one home to another is stressful for any dog, and if the Maltese who you have adopted went through trauma or neglect, then he will have even more to overcome.

Maltese are sensitive, loyal dogs who do not handle neglect or abandonment well. That said, these adoptable dogs have robust, bouncy personalities, which can recover from a lot with some time and attention. Here are some things to be aware of when adopting an adult Maltese, whether directly rehoming from an owner, adopting a rescue, or adopting from a breeder:

Photo Courtesy of Lu Crabtree

Past trauma

If your dog has gone through trauma in its past, then you are likely to see signs of this in all sorts of behaviors. Your dog may be easily startled by loud noises or any sign of anger in people in your home, even if you are only joking. You may find that your Maltese reacts unpredictably to normal household objects. A dog who has been hit with a rolled-up newspaper may respond fearfully or aggressively to newspapers from then on.

FUN FACT
Sugar the Maltese

Elizabeth Taylor owned a number of dogs during her life, but her most beloved was a Maltese named Sugar. Sugar was a nearly constant companion to Taylor, attending press conferences and photoshoots, until the dog died in 2005 at the age of 12. After Sugar's death, Taylor acquired two of Sugar's descendants, Delilah and Daisy.

Even an isolated event can cause trauma and ongoing phobia. If your Maltese is, for instance, nervous around doorways, it may be that he has been hit by a door or at some point ran into a glass door. Fearfulness in your new dog doesn't necessarily mean that he has been abused or neglected; it may just be a sign of an isolated traumatic event or an especially sensitive dog.

You will need to go very slowly with your Maltese as you help him overcome any past trauma. Often, the best solution is not to do anything but just be a calm and supportive force in your Maltese's life as he comes to grips with his new environment. Be sensitive to your dog's signals so that you will notice whenever a new phobia or past trauma comes to light.

Keep in mind that dogs generalize, so a dog that is afraid of an object or situation may also be afraid of similar objects or situations. It may be very difficult to figure out what the initial trigger or stressor might have been that caused your dog to be afraid of something, but truthfully, this isn't what matters. What is important is helping your dog to live a quality life, either despite his trauma or by helping him overcome it. As you get to know your dog better, provide lots of delicious treats and toys whenever he is near a fearful trigger or situation to help him overcome his phobias.

In my experience working at a rescue shelter, dogs almost always break through their trauma and adapt to their new environment. This speaks to the benevolence and good-heartedness of dogs. At the end of the day, they just want to be loved. Be patient with your dog's trauma and give it time to adapt. It's important not to force your dog into doing anything that it is afraid of.

Neglect

Neglect is not openly abusive or traumatic, and it may not always result in a dog who is scared of humans or household objects. However, a dog who has been neglected and has also suffered at the hands of humans may take some time to overcome his past experiences. With a breed that requires regular grooming like the Maltese, neglect often results in matted coats and long nails that grow into the paws. The pain that a Maltese may have gone through due to not being groomed may make him extremely fearful of grooming or even being touched.

Photo Courtesy of Talhia Rangel

Your dog may be very resistant to having his paws handled and may be unfamiliar with the standard practices of grooming. If your dog has been painfully groomed once becoming matted, he may become terrified or aggressive just at the sight of a brush. Most dogs can be rehabilitated from grooming neglect with patience and positive reinforcement, along with positive grooming experiences, but some dogs will always be very reactive to grooming tools, tables, and being groomed. If your dog simply cannot overcome his anxiety, then it may need to be sedated for grooming.

Adjusting to a new lifestyle

Wherever your Maltese lived before, whether he was a pampered house pet in a house full of other Maltese dogs at a breeder, loved by an older person who passed away, neglected in a home that didn't care about him, or kept like livestock for monetary breeding purposes without ever having the opportunity to bond with a human, all dogs have one thing in common when they come to live with you: they are in a brand new environment.

Some Maltese dogs settle smoothly into their new lives, while others take longer to adjust. The more similar your Maltese's old life was to your own, the easier it will be. Look for cues that your Maltese is trying to communicate with you and teach you about what he expects. Most importantly, be patient and don't force anything.

Your Maltese may dance by the door at a certain time, expectant of a walk that he used to get at that time. He may be hopeful every time you

Photo Courtesy of Laurie Mullins

Photo Courtesy of Yasemin Luca

get food out of the fridge or go to the kitchen if he is accustomed to receiving table scraps or treats from the kitchen.

Sometimes you will be able to maintain a routine that your Maltese is used to, while other habits may need to change. Regardless, it is very helpful for your Maltese if you pay attention and are aware of apparent expectations or confusion in your dog so that you can help him adapt to your lifestyle.

It's best to change your dog's habits through positive reinforcement rather than punishment. Your newly adopted dog may become afraid of you if you are too harshly punishing it right off of the bat. Try rewarding your dog for its positive behaviors rather than punishing it for its bad behaviors. This helps build trust between you and your new Maltese, especially if it lived in an abusive home prior.

What motivates your Maltese?

Everyone is motivated by something, including dogs. Some Maltese dogs are extremely food motivated, willing to do almost any kind of trick or behavior for a delectable treat. Other Maltese prefer to play over food and may be especially attached to particular toys or games. Still, other Maltese are more affectionate than they are playful or hungry and are more than willing to work just for indications of your love. It is important for you to learn what motivates your new Maltese if you are to train him and develop a positive working relationship with him. This is even more essential if you would like your Maltese to go places with you or if you want him to become a therapy animal to help other people.

Micah is almost completely food-driven. When a bag of food comes out of the pantry, he focuses entirely on the food. Nothing can phase or distract

Micah when food is on the table. I joke that he has a one-track mind when it comes to food. With this in mind, I have had the best luck training Micah with treats as a reward.

Offer your dog various treats, toys, and other potential motivators to see what makes him tick. Once you know what motivates your Maltese, it is very important to begin basic training. Whether or not you care that your dog can sit and stay or not, it is very important for dogs to develop the self-control to obey your commands.

This can be even more essential for a dog who has never received training before. Without any training, Maltese can become unruly and anxious. They may think that they need to tell you what's going on all the time, or they may become bored and pushy in trying to get your attention. A happy Maltese is a Maltese who has boundaries and understands his place in the family. Make sure that you learn what motivates your dog and use it to give your dog a framework of training, no matter how old he is when he comes to you.

Getting to know other pets

If you have other pets in your household, then your new Maltese will have more to adjust to than you, your home, and your lifestyle. Maltese are generally very social dogs who do well with other pets, including dogs, cats, and livestock. That said, any dog can be aggressive towards dogs or other animals.

If your Maltese has gone through some traumatic experience or been attacked by another animal in the past, he may have even more trouble with other animals. You should have found out from the breeder or the rescue whether a given dog is good with other animals.

Regardless of what a breeder says, it is essential that you go slowly and monitor all interactions between your new Maltese and your existing pets. Problems can happen faster than you may imagine, and signs that something isn't going right can be very subtle, so be sure to pay close attention and only allow your pets to interact when they can be supervised until you are confident that they are developing positive social relationships with one another.

Ask your breeder or rescue shelter if you can introduce the two pets before adopting. If they fight immediately, then you may want to consider a different dog. It's recommended that you introduce the two pets in a neutral space. This way, your current pet won't become territorial and aggressive. As with everything else, be patient and don't force any interactions. Let them figure it out themselves.

CHAPTER 5

Preparing for a Maltese Puppy

"Before bringing home your puppy, I always recommend that new owners have a nice sized indoor pen; large enough for a potty pad, bed, food, and toys. This gives their new puppy a safe place where they can go for quiet times or rest when needed."

SHARON PEARSON
Foxstone Maltese

The day that you learn when you'll be bringing home your Maltese puppy, your family is sure to be filled with excitement. You probably won't be able to tell which little bean in the litter is going to be yours from the others, but nonetheless, you drool over any picture the breeder sends. You may have weeks or months to prepare for your Maltese puppy to come home.

Regardless of how much time you have, it is essential that you take time to prepare for your Maltese puppy's homecoming. It's best to be prepared well before you bring home your new puppy. You'll need to do your best to prepare your family members, other pets, and home for the new addition to your family. Puppy-proofing and being prepared with the right equipment are essential in providing a safe and healthy living environment for your entire family.

HELPFUL TIP
The Maltese RX

The Maltese RX Newsletter is the official annual publication of the AMA. This newsletter is published yearly in winter and is available to AMA members and non-members. For more information about this publication, visit the AMA website at www.americanmaltese.org.

Briefing family members

Your family must be on the same page regarding your new Maltese before you bring your dog home. Any disagreements about training, feeding, and what the dog is and is not allowed to do should be worked out at this time. The entire family needs to be in agreement about how your Maltese lives with you. Otherwise, your Maltese will take advantage of inconsistencies to get what it wants. More importantly, your Maltese may become insecure without clear and consistent leadership from everyone in the family. Make sure that you are clear with your family about why it is important to be consistent for the dog's own benefit.

For example, consistencies are especially important when it comes to potty training. Each family member needs to be accountable to frequently let your new puppy outside to use the bathroom. Each family member needs to remain consistent in how to reward the puppy for going outside and remain consistent in how to discipline your puppy for going inside. It's important that you don't send mixed messages to your puppy.

Photo Courtesy of Ugnė Petrovaitė

Preparing other pets

If you have other pets in your home, then adding a new dog to the family will likely come as quite a surprise. Puppies get a lot of attention and take up a lot of energy. You don't want your current pets to feel jealous of the puppy or feel that its presence is interfering with their happiness.

Slowly reduce the time that you spend with current pets now so that they won't be shocked when a new Maltese arrives or associate their new reduced time with you with the new arrival. Get other pets used to staying out of the area where you will keep the puppy and set up equipment that you will use with the puppy, like a playpen.

It's recommended that you introduce your new puppy to your current pet in a neutral space, such as a dog park. This way, your two pets will get to know each other without the added layer of territorialism.

Puppy-proofing your home

"Be very sure not to leave anything within reach of a new puppy. Electrical cords, toxic plants, choke hazards; even a fall from a small child or larger dogs can be deadly to a Maltese puppy."

BARBARA SHEWMAKE
Storybook Maltese

Much like baby-proofing a house before you bring home a newborn, it's important to puppy-proof your house before bringing home a puppy. Puppies are curious by nature—and with that curiosity comes potentially destructive behavior that can cause your puppy harm. Young dogs are known for chewing on cords, getting into medications, falling down stairs, and more. Be sure to prepare your house to prevent damage to your belongings as well as your new family member.

One of the most dangerous things for a growing Maltese puppy is falling. Maltese are notorious for taking leaps that their little bodies cannot handle. Broken legs or other broken bones, sprains, neck, and back injuries are common as a result. You cannot assume that you can trust your puppy's depth perception to determine how far they can safely jump.

Maltese are well known for being fearless, willing to take a leap off of a bed or couch, even if it is much too tall for them. Maltese puppies are often too eager to use safer ways to get down, like provided stairs or ramps. Here are some things to look out for and ways to safeguard your new puppy and your belongings:

Photo Courtesy of Mary Lennon

Stairs

Stairs can be extremely dangerous for your Maltese puppy. Even a few stairs can cause a dangerous fall, especially if your puppy doesn't see them when running. Keep in mind that as a puppy, one single stair will be as tall as your Maltese. Each and every stair is a challenge that poses its own danger.

When you are teaching your Maltese to navigate stairs, start at the bottom of a landing and teach your dog to go up only the bottom stair or two at the beginning so that it doesn't tumble backward. One bad fall and your Maltese may become afraid of stairs, making it harder to train.

It's advised that you use baby gates to prevent your dog from falling down stairs while you're not around to supervise. Even if it's just one single stair from your kitchen into your living room, then it's advised to use a baby gate to prevent a fall.

At first, Micah struggled to learn how to navigate a staircase. He never really had much trouble going up the stairs, but going down was a different story. He would launch himself down the stairs rather than tackle one stair at a time. We set baby gates up to prevent Micah from accessing staircases when we weren't around to supervise.

Couches and beds

You are sure to want to put your Maltese puppy on the couch or bed to cuddle. Sitting on the couch with your puppy can suddenly become very dangerous if your puppy decides to leap off. There is no single tip for protecting your Maltese around couches and beds, but here are a few suggestions that may work well for your family:

- **MAKE YOUR BED INTO A CRIB:** If you want your Maltese puppy to sleep in the bed with you, then it is best to provide some kind of fencing around the bed to keep the dog from falling or jumping out. Your Maltese is unlikely to climb over even a small fence, so it doesn't have to be a significant border, but there should be some kind of barrier if you are going to have your Maltese in bed, especially if you're sleeping.
- **CREATE SOFT LANDINGS:** If you want to have your Maltese on the couch with you, keep a hand on them to prevent them from jumping off. As an added measure of precaution, you can use soft cushions and pillows on the floor so that if your Maltese does fall or jump off, they won't have as far to fall and will have a soft landing. Look at your couches and other

places where you may want to sit with your Maltese and think about what you can provide to offer a soft landing.

- **USE SOFT CRATES:** One of the best ways to enjoy having your puppy with you while also keeping them safe is to use a soft, collapsible crate on the furniture. Your puppy will have their own little spot in the crate where you can pet them and play with them, but they will be restricted from falling off, and you can easily close the crate door if you need to get up and leave for a minute.

Other puppy-proofing ideas

Here are a few things that you'll need to do to puppy-proof your home.

- **COVER CORDS AND OUTLETS.** Puppies often seem to be irresistibly drawn to chewing on electrical cords and playing around electrical outlets. Make sure that all of your outlets have secure covers that your puppy will be unable to open. Keep cords covered with puppy-safe housing or run them well above where your puppy can reach.
- **POISONS AND TOXINS.** Do your research to find out what is poisonous and toxic to dogs. Chemicals like household cleaners, roach and rat poison, and other clearly dangerous chemicals should be kept in a cabinet, well away from where your Maltese puppy can reach. However, you may be surprised to learn that some seemingly innocuous items like sugar-free gum can also be deadly for your puppy. Things like medications, bleach, and chocolate should be stored safely away from where your puppy can reach them.
- **MOVE PLANTS OUT OF THE WAY.** If there are plants that your puppy might be able to reach, it is best to move them out of reach. Most puppies find plants irresistible, and a majority of house plants are at least somewhat poisonous. To the tiny Maltese, any kind of toxin can be extremely dangerous. Remember that fallen leaves can also be dangerous for your dog. Consider buying only pet-safe plants, particularly plants without needles like cacti or other pointed succulents, to prevent injury.
- **TREAT AND SEAL FLOORS.** Let's face it; your puppy is probably going to have a few potty-training accidents. It's a good idea to take care of your floors before you bring your Maltese home so that any accidents won't be too damaging. You may want to protect your floor with puppy pads in rooms where your new family member will be spending a lot of time.

Puppy pads are scented, absorbent pads that can be placed indoors and that encourage your dog to relieve themselves on them. This way, any indoor potty accidents end up on the pad rather than your flooring. It's also advised that you keep your new puppy off of carpeted surfaces until they are properly trained. Flooring such as vinyl is ideal for potty training, as it's easy to clean and won't absorb any odors.

Equipment

Maltese are small dogs that are quite easy to live with from the very beginning. That said, there is some equipment that is important for you to have for your Maltese before you bring them home.

Harness and leash

Maltese are tiny as puppies, but they grow quickly. So choose a highly adjustable harness that is specifically made for tiny dogs. The more padding and webbing you can find, the better. Your Maltese will have to learn how to walk in a harness. They tend to be extremely enthusiastic little dogs, and they can hurt themselves on a harness that is too restrictive or a harness that puts pressure on the neck.

Maltese should never be walked on a collar, as they can have a prevalence towards neck and back problems that are easily aggravated by a collar. The leash that you use won't need to be very strong since your Maltese puppy will be very small, but it should be easy to hold onto.

Maltese have a tendency to not pull on the leash at all until they want something, and then they pull suddenly, which can make it easy for you to lose hold of the leash. So, get a leash that is easy to slip over your wrist.

Never use a retractable leash with your Maltese, as the sudden pressure can make it much easier to hurt your Maltese's neck or back, even if you use a harness.

Micah wears a harness every time he goes potty outside or on a walk. Another benefit of using a harness is that you don't have to take it off every time the dog goes outside. If you purchase a high-quality harness that fits your dog well, then they won't even notice that they're wearing it. Be sure to use the adjustable straps on the harness so that it fits snuggly but not too tight. Make sure there is at least a finger width of wiggle room in between the harness and your dog's body.

Food and treats

Choose food that is specifically designed for small breed puppies. It is important that your Maltese not gain too much weight, especially when they are growing. So be sure to choose food that is nutritious but not overly fattening.

It is best for Maltese puppies to have glucosamine, chondroitin, and other joint supplements throughout their puppyhood so that they develop strong joints that will continue to support them through life.

It is up to you whether you want to choose a dog food that is formulated with joint supplements or choose treats with supplements. Whatever treats you choose for your Maltese should be highly nutritious and ideally deliver additional vitamins and minerals.

Photo Courtesy of Leona Lupulesku Leona's Maltese

Micah takes a daily joint Omega-3 joint supplement. Maltese and other small dog breeds are known to develop hip problems later in life. Their small stature makes it harder on their joints when absorbing the impact of jumping up and down furniture. Micah also hikes with us and jumps up and down rocks and boulders along the path. The joint supplements should help his hips stay healthy for years to come.

Dried fruit like apple and banana, dried sweet potato, dried fish, freeze-dried tendons and esophagus, and other natural treats are all great options for your Maltese puppy. Make sure you choose foods that are relatively easy to chew but still provide a challenge to occupy your Maltese. It is best not to choose any food or treats that are very mushy or wet, as these tend to end up in your Maltese's hair on the paws and muzzle.

Bones and other chewable treats will come in handy when your puppy starts to teethe. Dental bones will help keep your puppy's breath fresh while easing the pain of the teething process. Avoid all rawhide bones as they pose a choking and digestion hazard.

Toys

Maltese tend to be very playful dogs, and many enjoy playing with a wide range of toys. Many Maltese like fetch toys such as balls and large plush toys that they can shake around. Puppies are especially fond of large plush toys, which may be comforting as a replacement for littermates and mom.

Below is a list of toys that your Maltese is sure to love:

- **BALLS:** These toys have been a fan-favorite of Maltese for years. A ball that bounces and rolls like a tennis ball triggers a primal instinct in your Maltese, and the chase begins. Look for mini tennis balls or softer balls that are adequately sized for your Maltese.
- **ROPE TOYS:** Rope toys are ideal for bonding with your Maltese and ultimately burning some of their puppy energy. Be gentle when playing tug-of-war so that you don't damage your puppy's sensitive teeth.
- **STUFFED TOYS:** Stuffed toys offer the best of both worlds. You can either play fetch or play tug-of-war. Stuffed toys are soft and squishy, which provides peace of mind when playing tug-of-war. The softness of this toy will ensure that your puppy's mouth doesn't get damaged.
- **CHEW TOYS:** It's in your dog's nature to want to chew on things, particularly when its teething. A chew toy can be thrown for a game of fetch or played with solo when you're out of the house. It's a great toy to have around while you're at work. Encouraging your dog to chew on a

chew toy makes it less likely that your Maltese will chew on your sofa or bedpost.

Micah's two favorite toys are chew toys and stuffed toys. He loves to play tug-of-war with his stuffed toy. He loves his chew toys even more than his stuffed toys and is almost always carrying one around in his mouth.

Playpen and crate

A playpen and crate will be invaluable in your life with your Maltese. As much as you would surely like to spend every minute of your day watching and playing with your puppy, this is simply not realistic or even good for your dog. Your Maltese should spend time away from you and by themselves.

Playpens are essential for giving your puppy some freedom while also restricting their movements and keeping them from getting into anything that they shouldn't. A crate is important for potty training, and collapsible crates can be very useful when you want to put your puppy on the sofa or the bed. Portable backpack-style crates can also be great for taking your puppy with you before they are fully vaccinated so that they won't catch anything by being on the ground.

The size of the crate is also important. It should be large enough that the puppy can stand up and turn around but small enough to prevent any potty accidents. By nature, dogs and other animals rarely poopy or potty where they sleep. A smaller-sized crate will help train your puppy on how to hold its potty until it is taken outside. If you're worried about your puppy outgrowing its crate, then look for a large crate with a divider and remove the divider once your dog grows.

Wire crates are preferred over plastic crates as they are collapsible and can be easily stored. They also have more visibility than plastic crates, so your puppy can see outside of the crate. Wire crates are also more customizable in size and oftentimes come with a divider. Lastly, wire crates typically come with plastic flooring, so it's easy to clean if there is an accident.

Grooming equipment

Grooming will be a part of your life with your Maltese from the day you bring him home. It is imperative to acclimate your Maltese puppy to bathing and grooming tools and routines from the beginning. Choose gentle tools that are designed for a puppy's delicate hair and skin. Here are a few basic tools that you should have on hand when you bring home your Maltese puppy:

- **SNUB NOSE SCISSORS.** Scissors without sharp ends are useful for all kinds of situations, like when your puppy has dragged its tail through gum. Scissors can also be useful for little touch-ups between major grooming.
- **DETANGLING BRUSH.** A straightforward detangling brush designed for longer hair is essential for everyday brushing to keep your Maltese tangle-free. Even if your Maltese is clipped quite short, it's a good idea to have a detangling brush on hand, especially for the ears and tail, which are usually a bit longer.
- **GROOMING WIPES.** Many Maltese have a tendency to have a little bit of drainage and staining around the eyes, so it's a good idea to have grooming wipes on hand so that you can clean your dog's face daily. These wipes are also very convenient for cleaning up after your Maltese has eaten something messy and for wiping down the coat if it has gotten a little bit dirty, but you aren't ready to bathe your dog yet.
- **PUPPY SHAMPOO.** Choose a gentle puppy shampoo for your Maltese. It's not a bad idea to choose a whitening shampoo so that your puppy will stay sparkly white from the beginning. Whether you choose whitening or not, make sure that it is specifically a puppy shampoo—not a human shampoo—designed not to irritate your puppy's eyes or skin.
- **NAIL CLIPPERS.** It is important to clip your puppy's nails frequently, especially since very few Maltese are active enough to wear down the nails naturally. Most Maltese puppies do well with rounded puppy nail clippers.

CHAPTER 6

Bringing Home Your Maltese Puppy

"A new owner of a Maltese puppy may be surprised to learn that they 'graze' throughout the day. They'll often pick up a few kibbles and haul them off to their bed or favorite hiding place and nibble them. Only a puppy that has been starved will stand at the bowl and gobble down their food. This is why it's important to keep food available to the Maltese puppy at all times."

BARBARA SHEWMAKE
Storybook Maltese

HELPFUL TIP
Sleep Safety

The first few nights with a new puppy can sometimes be the most challenging while your puppy acclimates to a bed that isn't shared with their littermates. Many dog owners are tempted to bring the puppy into bed for everyone to get some sleep, but due to Maltese puppies' small size, the height of the bed can pose an injury risk if the puppy falls. A safe way to keep the puppy close for the first few days is to place the puppy's crate or kennel directly onto the bed, ensuring that the crate can not fall or be knocked over during the night. If this can't be accomplished safely, placing the crate close by can also help reduce anxiety for the first few nights.

The day that you bring home your new Maltese puppy will doubtless be a day that you'll remember forever. Your family will have been looking forward to this day and preparing for some time.

Surely, you'll have a hard time sleeping the night before you go to pick up your new pup. Bringing your Maltese puppy home is naturally extremely exciting, but it is also an essential time in your relationship with your dog. You don't want to do anything at this time that doesn't set your puppy up for success. Here's what you need to know about bringing home your Maltese puppy.

Photo Courtesy of Gabriele Puplauskaite

Picking up your Maltese puppy

The excitement of picking up a new puppy is unlike any other. Be sure that your judgment is not clouded by excitement and come prepared. Picking your puppy up for the first time can be stressful on the little nugget. It's likely that you'll be separating your new puppy from its mom and siblings. This is a traumatic and stressful event for your puppy, so be prepared for it to whine and cry while it deals with its separation anxiety. During this time, it's important to remain compassionate. Don't scold your puppy for whining. It's scared! Instead, try to comfort it.

For the drive home, be sure that you're prepared with a crate or box that can be buckled with a seatbelt. The crate should be lined with blankets to make your new puppy as comfortable as possible. The blankets will also be easy to clean in case your new puppy has an accident.

Resist the urge to allow the puppy to ride home on your lap or sitting freely on the car seat or floorboard. For starters, it's dangerous if you get into an accident. It's also not advised because of potty accidents. Cleaning potty out of your car is much more difficult than cleaning potty out of your home. Therefore, it's advised that you keep your puppy in its crate until you're home.

Getting to know each other

There is something undeniably strange about the moment you bring your new Maltese puppy into your home, and you regard each other as dog and dog parent for the first time. Maltese are naturally gregarious and outgoing. Assuming that your breeder has socialized the puppy properly, your Maltese should be excited to get to know you and happy to meet your family.

However, you should expect some anxiety as well. Your puppy will be in a strange place away from his family for the very first time. It will be exciting for your puppy but also scary. Here is how to get to know each other at the beginning.

Photo Courtesy of Melina Dillard

First days

You may want to show your new adorable puppy off to all of your friends, but for the first few days at home, it is best to keep him calm, quiet, and away from any more activity than is absolutely necessary. You want to get to know your puppy yourself before you begin introducing them to everybody else. You don't yet know what your puppy may be scared of, what they like, and what they don't like. You want to have that information before you expose them to new situations.

For the first couple of days that you have your puppy, live quietly together. Take time to get to know one another. Spend lots of time just being together, working on simple training, playing, and building your bond. Maltese love most people, but they tend to form an intense bond with their family. Take this time to begin to build that bond.

Sleeping arrangements

For many people, sleeping arrangements are one of the more challenging aspects of bringing home a new Maltese puppy. Maltese are loving dogs who want to be with you all of the time.

Furthermore, your Maltese will have just been separated from their family, so they'll be feeling especially needy. You may want to have your puppy on the bed with you, but there is a risk that they could fall off and get injured. You have a couple of options for sleeping arrangements with your new Maltese puppy:

On the floor

It may take some time to teach your Maltese to be happy without making physical contact with you while you're sleeping, but being in the room can make a big difference. It also helps to give your Maltese puppy something with your scent and something with the scent of the mother or littermate if possible.

Warm water bottles or devices designed to comfort puppies can also make a big difference for this sensitive breed. If your puppy whines, you can be right there to comfort them, but also be firm that the puppy is not allowed to be on the bed with you while sleeping.

We tried forcing Micah to sleep on the floor in a crate when he was a puppy, and he hated it. Micah would bark and whine the entire night, and we couldn't get any sleep. He would stop whining as soon as we picked him up and allowed him to sleep in our bed. If you don't want your puppy sleeping in your bed with you, then be prepared for some long nights of whining and barking.

In a crate on the bed

Another option for sleeping with your Maltese puppy is to put a crate on the bed. This is really the only safe way that you can have a Maltese puppy in the bed with you without any danger of rolling over on them or risking the puppy falling off the bed and onto the floor. There's still some risk of you knocking the crate down, but in general, most people can find a way to secure a crate on the bed in a way that it won't fall off.

Soft crates work best for this. By setting your Maltese puppy up in this way, you can keep your puppy close to you, reach out and touch him, and get accustomed to having them in your bed without the risk of injury. As your dog gets older and learns how to navigate your bed more easily, you can graduate to having your dog sleep in the bed with you without a crate. However, when your dog is a very small puppy, the crate is advised.

Fence in your bed

The final option should already have been considered before now since it takes a bit more work. You can make your bed into a crib, ensuring that your Maltese puppy won't fall out. This doesn't protect your pup if you roll over on them, but if you're confident that this won't be a problem for you, fencing in your bed might be your best solution.

When Micah was a puppy, we immediately caved in and allowed him to sleep in our bed. We chose to create a pillow perimeter around the bed to ensure that he didn't fall off. We also tried to keep him separated from us with pillows so that we wouldn't accidentally roll over onto him at night.

Bathroom breaks

You won't be getting much sleep with a new Maltese puppy in the house. Their tiny stature means that food and water run through their digestive system faster than normal. Maltese puppies will most likely have to be taken out once every hour throughout the entire night. If you refuse to take your puppy out in the middle of the night, then be prepared to clean up potty in the morning. You'll also be developing bad habits in your dog.

Be observant for signs that your Maltese has to go potty. Signs include restlessness and whimpering. Taking your puppy out to go potty will help prevent whimpering and help everyone in the house get a better night of sleep.

Beginning basic training

More advanced training techniques such as tricks will be touched on later in the book, but it's important to begin training your Maltese as soon as you bring them home. Every aspect of your life with your Maltese involves communication and, therefore, training. Your dog needs to learn what appropriate behavior is in a wide range of situations. It is much harder for a puppy to unlearn a bad habit than to learn it right the first time.

You won't do your Maltese puppy any favors by delaying training. Maltese are generally eager-to-please and willing to learn, but they can be a bit on the stubborn side as well. The earlier you establish training and the kind of expectations that you have of your Maltese, the easier it will be for your dog to fit into your lifestyle. Here are a few aspects of training that should start right at the beginning.

Photo Courtesy of Joan Ryan

Self-control

It is believed that the Roman emperor Claudius and Roman governor of Malta, Publius, both owned Maltese dogs.

One of the hardest things for any young dog is controlling their impulses. Maltese don't feel lots of strong instincts like prey drive, herding drive, or the drive to protect people or properties, like some other breeds. This means that it can be a little bit easier to train them.

That said, there are plenty of things a Maltese might want to do that you may not want them to do. Teaching your young dog self-control is absolutely essential, right from the beginning.

Thankfully, self-control training is incredibly easy. It just takes steady and consistent training for your puppy to develop the self-control they need to be a happy and well-adjusted pet. Here is how to perform self-control training with your Maltese puppy.

- **"LOOK AT ME."** Ask your puppy to look at you, using the command of your choosing. When they do, give them a treat. Keep working on this command until your Maltese looks at you every time you ask them to.
- **STAY.** Many people make the mistake of thinking they need to train a dog to sit or lie down before they teach it to stay. In fact, you want your dog to think about the command to stay independently of these other commands. After giving your dog the "look at me" command, tell them to stay and wait an instant before giving them the treat.
- **INCREASE STAYS.** Increase the time that you make your puppy wait after you tell them to look at you before you give the treat. The goal is to teach your puppy to remain centered on looking at you for as long as it takes to get the reward.
- **REMIND WHEN YOUR PUPPY BREAKS.** As you stretch out the time that your puppy waits, they will surely become distracted. Harsh discipline is never a good training tactic, but you do need to point out that your dog is not performing the desired task. Simply remind your puppy to look at you again and reduce the time they are waiting for a bit until they have developed the self-control for the longer wait.
- **KEEP TRAINING.** Many people stop working on increasing their dog's stay once their dog can wait for a few seconds. However, your Maltese has

the intelligence to develop much better self-control than this. The better your dog's self-control, the less likely they will be to develop hyperactivity issues. Great self-control training can even make separation anxiety less likely. Keep encouraging a puppy to stay for longer and longer waits, even as much as five or ten minutes, with a motivating reward.

Ramps and stairs

You should immediately start teaching your puppy the proper way to get on and off furniture.

Make sure ramps and stairs are secure. The slightest amount of instability in the stairs or ramp that you ask your puppy to use may cause anxiety about using them in the future. Make sure that your equipment is extremely sturdy and solid and doesn't move an inch or wiggle at all when your puppy steps on it.

- **LURE WITH TREATS.** The best way to teach your Maltese puppy to go up and down ramps or stairs is to lure him with a treat. Simply hold the treat in front of your puppy's mouth and ask them to come. It's not a bad idea to give a couple of rewards just for touching the ramp, another reward for standing entirely on it, and so on, especially if your puppy seems to be anxious.
- **ENFORCE USE.** If your puppy asks to get up on the couch when the ramp is available, tell your puppy to use the ramp instead of picking them up. If your puppy ever tries to get off the couch, bed, or go down the stairs without using the ramp, gently correct them and reinforce the way you want them to use the equipment.
- **SAFETY BACKUPS.** Again, it is extremely dangerous for your puppy to fall, especially when they are young. Use a secure harness and leash to train your puppy so that if they fall, you will be able to guide them gently to the ground. If you're going to have your puppy on the sofa with you, have lots of pillows on the ground. Whenever you're training your puppy to go up and down stairs and ramps, make sure that there are safety backups to keep your dog from getting injured.

Basic obedience

Your puppy should learn the basics like sit, down, come, and some tricks as well. Maltese are eager to learn, and on average, they are much happier pets when they have some training. Most Maltese puppies are especially eager to learn new tricks, although they might be less excited about behavior modification like learning not to bark.

Tips for training basic obedience

- **VARY YOUR TRAINING ROUTINE.** Your Maltese will quickly learn the schedule if you always do commands in the same order. Make sure that your Maltese is really learning the commands and not performing a song-and-dance for a treat by varying commands whenever you train.
- **REPEAT TRAINING FREQUENTLY IN VARIED SITUATIONS.** Just because a dog learns a command in one situation doesn't mean they'll remember it in another. Train your Maltese puppy in as many different conditions and circumstances as possible so that they will thoroughly internalize the training.
- **USE HAND COMMANDS.** People are verbally focused, and we tend to think only about the voice commands that we are using when we train dogs. However, dogs tend to be more physically oriented. Your Maltese is very likely to pick up on training more quickly if you use both a hand command and a verbal command. As an added benefit, you'll then be able to use either the hand command or the verbal command when you want to ask your dog to do something.

Down

Down is a critical command to learn for when you have guests over. Puppies often have a hard time controlling their excited energy, and they jump all over guests or other animals. This command also comes in handy when training your puppy to stay off the furniture. Use a stern voice and a hand gesture to indicate that what they're doing is wrong. To start, you'll have to use your hand to gently push your puppy down as you tell them "Down." until they learn the command.

Drop it

Another critical command is teaching your dog to "Drop it." This especially comes in handy during the teething phase when your puppy wants to chew on just about everything. Use a stern voice and a hand gesture to tell your dog to drop it. In the beginning, you'll have to remove the item from your dog's mouth while saying "Drop it." until they learn the command.

Sit

Hold a treat just over your Maltese's nose and slowly move it back towards their tail. If your Maltese jumps up or walks backward, start over again. When done properly, your Maltese's nose will follow the treat upwards, and their hind end will end up on the ground. When this happens, say the command, "sit," and give your puppy the treat. Keep practicing until you no longer have to lure your puppy with a treat to ask them to sit.

Lay down

Lay down is most easily learned after sit. From a sitting position, lure your dog's nose down with a treat. Sometimes it is helpful to put a little gentle pressure on your dog's back so that they understand you want them to lie and not to crouch. Once your dog has accomplished a down from a sit, work on asking them to go down from a stand.

Stand

Many people overlook teaching their dogs to stand since that is usually the position dogs are in when the training starts. However, if you want your dog to break the sit or stay, it is much better to ask them to stand than to simply let them move out of a sit or stay on their own. This will help them to learn that they aren't supposed to break a sit or down until they're released.

Tricks

There are all kinds of tricks you can teach your Maltese to do. Spinning in a circle is a popular trick, which many Maltese learn to do on their own when they want to express excitement. You can also teach your Maltese to jump on their hind legs or offer you a paw. These are clever dogs who enjoy learning physical tricks. For all tricks, the best way is to teach your Maltese by luring them with a treat. If a trick is complicated, it is best to break it up into pieces. For instance, if you're going to teach your Maltese to spin in a circle, you can first reward them for turning around and then reward them for completing the circle. It's a good habit to use small-sized training treats to prevent your puppy from putting on too much weight.

Manage relationships with people and other pets

Maltese are gregarious dogs who tend to get along very well with everybody. They're well known for being fearless for their size and unworried about meeting new people or animals regardless of size. However, Maltese can also be quite yappy if they aren't trained properly. To set your Maltese up for success, you'll want to manage their relationships with people and other pets.

Meeting new people

Maltese generally like to meet new people, but your Maltese puppy may be a bit hesitant or standoffish at first. Lots of barking, sometimes with a lot of intensity that is difficult to curb, is not uncommon either. You want to teach your Maltese to meet people the right way.

- **ENCOURAGE BOLDNESS.** You want your Maltese to walk right up to your guests and say hello, not pace back and forth anxiously. Put a bowl of treats by the door and encourage your guests to give your Maltese a treat as soon as they walk in. That way, your Maltese will learn to meet guests happily instead of being standoffish.
- **REWARD ALLOWING PICKING UP.** Maltese may be nervous about being picked up by new people. Give your dog a great treat when he allows himself to be picked up by somebody new.
- **BACK UP YOUR GUEST'S COMMANDS.** You want your Maltese to learn to listen to your guests. If your guest encourages your Maltese to stop jumping up or tells them to come, back up their requests by asking your dog to do the same thing and rewarding them for doing it.
- **CONTROL YOUR GUEST'S BEHAVIOR.** Naturally, if your dog is dropped, this can be extremely dangerous and traumatizing. However, being picked up quickly or without warning, handled roughly, and a number of other behaviors on the part of your guests can also affect your dog. Teach your guests how to properly pick up your dog, and make sure that they give your dog warning before doing so. Be very clear that your Maltese is not a toy but an animal that requires respect and that you will protect.

Meeting other pets

Maltese generally get along very well with other animals. They are typically good with dogs and cats, and many are just fine with small household animals like rabbits and birds as well. They don't tend to have a particularly strong prey drive. Because they are courageous little dogs, most aren't overwhelmingly scared of larger pets either. Most of the time, your efforts in controlling relationships between your other pets and your Maltese will be on the part of the other pet.

To properly introduce your new puppy to other dogs, it's important that you do it in a neutral space. If there is another animal already living in your house, then you should introduce them in a neutral spot such as a dog park or in the neighborhood on a walk. Pets are territorial by nature and may feel intimidated by a new dog in the house. Introducing them in a neutral spot gives them time to warm up to each other before forcing them to share a space.

Be very observant for signs of aggression, such as deep growling and snarling. If either pet shows their teeth, then it's a sign that things aren't going well. Don't be discouraged by this. Just be sure to keep distance between the two and give them time to warm up to each other. Having both pets leashed will help separate the two if things go south.

Larger dogs can very easily injure a Maltese without meaning to. Even a large cat can seriously hurt your Maltese puppy if they are not very careful. Never leave your Maltese unsupervised with other pets, no matter how well they're getting along. Puppy behavior often changes suddenly. You don't want to take a chance with a change happening that causes aggression in another pet while you're not there.

Larger pets should be avoided altogether unless necessary. Dog parks, for example, have "small breed" and "large breed" sections. Make sure to stay exclusively within the "small breed" section. At the dog park, it's advised that you keep your puppy close to you and observe how other dogs are behaving. Stay away from the dogs with too high energy or dogs that seem to be aggressive.

When your Maltese is playing with other pets, be aware of the interactions and interfere if necessary. Teach pets to play gently together. If anyone yelps or the play gets too aggressive or intense, intervene. It is your responsibility to teach your pets how to play with your Maltese and keep your Maltese from being injured.

Photo Courtesy of Angela Hay

First vet visit

You will probably bring your Maltese puppy to the vet not long after bringing them home. You want to make sure that your puppy is completely healthy, and they'll probably need a booster vaccination soon after arriving at your home as well.

What to expect

On your puppy's first vet visit, your veterinarian will give them a full physical. They'll check the heart, lungs, ears, joints, etc. Your veterinarian will check the records provided by the breeder and provide any vaccinations that your puppy needs. They may talk to you about optional vaccinations that may only be needed if your puppy has access to standing water or wildlife.

Your veterinarian is also a great source of information for tips on grooming, how to keep your puppy's eyes stain-free, etc. Be sure to take your time to thoroughly talk to your veterinarian about potential health risks for your puppy and what you should do to keep them healthiest.

Making the first vet visit a good experience for your puppy

The first vet visit is important in establishing a positive relationship between your puppy and the vet. Talk to your veterinarian about what the experience will be like and what your puppy can expect. Make sure you bring your puppy's favorite toys and treats to make the experience as pleasant as possible.

If you can, it's great to combine the first vet visit with another very pleasant experience, like meeting another nice dog in the lobby. Your dog is certain to have a few unpleasant experiences at the vet at some point, so you want to counteract those experiences with as many pleasant experiences as possible. Now is not the time to hold back with treats. Bring the food your dog likes the best and give them plenty of it while at the vet.

First groomer visit

Many Maltese owners choose to take care of grooming themselves, but many others choose to delegate this important responsibility to a professional. If you'll be letting a groomer handle most of your Maltese's grooming care, you may only need to brush your dog to keep mats from forming between groomer visits.

You want your Maltese to have a good relationship with the groomer; otherwise, this will be an unpleasant monthly experience. Here is how to set your puppy up for success with their first visit to the groomer.

Pick a great groomer

The groomer that you choose matters. A lot. Your groomer doesn't just have to know how to cut and style your Maltese's hair. They are responsible for making grooming a pleasant experience for your dog.

Get references and talk to your groomer at length about how they deal with dogs misbehaving, what they do to achieve certain cuts, and what their standard procedures are. If you get a bad feeling, look elsewhere. Many groomers won't let you in their studio while they're working, but they should be open about letting you see where dogs are kept and where the work is done.

They should seem to have a good relationship with the animals. Dogs should not cower away from the groomer or resist being taken out of the crate. The groomer should be happy to talk with you and willing to take time to make sure that your mind is at ease about your puppy's care. Ideally, the first visit to the groomer will not involve much grooming.

Your groomer can take time to get acquainted with your dog and introduce them to the grooming tools, table, and environment. Be sure to pay and tip your groomer appropriately for this extra time.

Make grooming day a great day

You want every day that your puppy goes to the groomer to be an especially good day in as many ways as possible. Make sure your puppy gets some exercise to get the wiggles out, but not so much exercise that they are exhausted on the grooming table. A great solution is to give your puppy a very engaging food toy that they'll enjoy. This way, you can give your Maltese some physical exercise and mental stimulation and also reduce their breakfast so they won't have to go potty while at the groomer.

Be sure that you have a positive attitude when you bring your dog to the groomer. If you're anxious, your puppy is likely to pick up on that anxiety as well. Be positive and outgoing about the experience, and your Maltese probably will be as well. Remember, this is a very sensitive breed and is highly able to pick up on your moods.

Watch your Maltese after grooming

Keep an eye on your puppy when they come home from the groomer. Sometimes the signs of a stressful or anxiety-provoking experience are quite subtle. It is normal for your puppy to be sleepier than normal and to lick at any areas that have had work done.

However, if your dog is lethargic, seems frightened, or isn't interested in the usual activities, you may question whether they had a traumatizing experience at the groomer. If you have any suspicions that your groomer treated your dog roughly, insist that you watch the grooming next time or find a new groomer.

Micah's grooming experiences

Finding a good groomer for Micah was an uphill battle. Each groomer that we tried told us that Micah didn't like his rear end being groomed, which made it difficult for the groomer to do their job. In addition, most groomers did a terrible job on Micah's eyes. We had to constantly remind our groomers to pay special attention to cleaning his tear stains.

Micah would sometimes walk abnormally after a visit to the groomer and would be constantly scratching. It was clear that he was uncomfortable. We now request our groomers to use a special shampoo for sensitive skin since Maltese have a history of having sensitive skin.

We also learned that Micah was suffering from clipper burn in certain areas. Clipper burn happens when groomers let the clippers get too hot and burns the skin of your dog. If your dog is noticeably uncomfortable after a visit to the groomer, then it's possible that it is suffering from clipper burn.

To prevent clipper burn altogether, we now request that Micah only gets his hair cut with sheers. We don't allow groomers to use clippers. Ever since this switch, coupled with the switch to a sensitive shampoo, Micah has had no issues with the groomer whatsoever.

CHAPTER 7
Raising Your Maltese

Getting to know your Maltese better as they become an established part of your life is a lot of fun. It also comes with some challenges as you teach your puppy how to live in your world. Maltese are very trainable and devoted to their people, but they have bouts of stubbornness.

Your puppy may show unexpected behavior as they develop. Sometimes it feels like just as you're getting to know your Maltese, they seem to turn into an entirely different dog. This is completely normal for any breed, including the Maltese.

It is important not to set your expectations too high and to maintain physical control of your puppy as they get older. Many adult Maltese can be trusted off-leash in lots of situations and in the house, but it takes some time to get there.

Here's what you need to know about the joyful but sometimes challenging period between puppyhood and adulthood.

Photo Courtesy of HeatherAnn Goodrich

Satisfying instincts

Your Maltese is not a blank slate. Certain things will be inherently appealing to them. Understanding what your Maltese is likely to want and how to satisfy their desires is the best way to avoid destructive behavior.

Perhaps more importantly, effectively meeting your dog's instinctual needs shows them that you can provide positive reinforcement in a variety of appealing ways. This makes training much easier, especially with a breed that can tend to choose their own desires over following your commands.

Chewing

One of the most essential instincts of any puppy is chewing. Chewing helps to relieve pain and pressure while teething. It is also a stress reliever and entertainment when your dog is bored. Chewing will help to strengthen your puppy's teeth and remove plaque and tartar.

Providing the right things for your Maltese to chew on is essential, both for healthy development and to make sure that they don't use those sharp puppy teeth on your furniture. These are some tips to help you keep your Maltese from chewing on things they shouldn't.

Variety

Too often, pet parents get their puppy a chew toy or two and consider the job done. However, puppies crave variety. An intelligent puppy like a Maltese wants to understand as many different textures and sensations as possible.

Furthermore, teething puppies tend to explore chewing possibilities in an attempt to relieve pain and pressure. Here is some of the variety you ought to give your teething puppy.

- **NYLON BONES.** Nylon bones are still a standard for puppies. Choose varieties that are made specifically for small-breed puppies, and make sure that only tiny slivers come off when your dog chews.
- **KONG TOYS AND OTHER FOOD DISTRIBUTING TOYS.** Food distributing toys like the classic Kong for puppies are perfect for entertaining your dog while you stretch out mealtime. A Maltese puppy's tiny body doesn't need much food, so stretching out meals with a food toy is a great way to encourage positive mouth health and also entertain with food.
- **FROZEN FRUITS AND VEGETABLES.** Fruits and vegetables are healthy treats for your puppy. Freezing them is a great way to soothe sore puppy teeth.

- **NATURAL CHEWS.** Natural chews that are soft enough for your puppy's teeth, like esophagus, tendon, and bully sticks, are an excellent source of chondroitin and glucosamine. These joint supplements are important for your puppy's developing joints as well as being great for the teeth.

Supervision

Even if you give your puppy every chew toy known to dog-kind, they will still be tempted to find out what your furniture feels like on their teeth. It is not intuitive for a puppy to understand what they should and should not chew on. It is up to you to supervise your puppy and correct and redirect them if they chew on inappropriate objects.

Always have a couple of good toys handy to give your puppy as an alternative to the inappropriate item they want to chew on. If you can't supervise your puppy, leave them in a contained area with toys where they cannot access things they should not chew on.

Dedication

It feels very natural to supervise your puppy for the first week or two that they're home, but as your puppy gets older and you settle into a routine, it can become too easy to forget about your puppy for a few minutes while you do the dishes or settle into a television show. However, puppies are constantly finding new ways to challenge their environment and get into things they shouldn't.

You may not realize that your puppy has been chewing at the back leg of your couch until they have already done significant damage. You might not notice that your puppy has found access to an electrical cord until they are injured. Therefore, it's important to stick to your supervision routine until your dog is mentally mature.

FUN FACT
Breed Popularity

In 1888 the Maltese was recognized as a breed by the American Kennel Club (AKC) and, as of 2021, is the 37th most popular breed registered with the AKC. In 1877, this breed was shown at the first annual Westminster Kennel Club Dog Show in New York as the Maltese Lion Dog.

Chasing and Searching

Maltese do not have a very high prey drive compared to many other types of dogs, but many individuals do still feel the desire to chase things, especially smaller things. You can have fun with this instinct by playing games with your dog. Unless you have control of this instinct, you won't be able to trust your dog off-leash in any circumstances.

No matter how well your Maltese is trained, you should never allow your dog off-leash where traffic or other dangers are near. Well-trained Maltese can often be trusted under supervision off-leash in safe places. Dogs who have learned not to give in to their chase and search instincts are much safer off the lead. Here are some positive ways to engage your Maltese's chase and search instincts.

Fetch

Fetch is a straightforward way to engage your puppy's desire to chase something. Teaching your Maltese to bring something back encourages them to learn to love you. It creates a fun game that you'll have for the rest of your life together.

If your puppy is reluctant to bring back the toy, try giving them a food reward for bringing it back. Soon your puppy will learn that bringing back the toy is what you want and that there is a reward for them in giving it up.

Some puppies learn well if you put treats inside of the toy and then help your puppy get to them when they bring it back. Experiment with ways to reward your puppy for bringing back a toy to give them outlets for their chasing instincts.

Micah has never been great at fetch. He's good at chasing the toy and picking it up—but almost never brings it back. Micah likes when I chase him around the house to get the toy back rather than bringing it back to me.

Find the treat or toy

Many Maltese absolutely love this game, which allows them to follow their nose and use their minds to search a space for something they really want to find. If your puppy isn't extremely interested in toys, this game can also be done with a treat. Sometimes, starting with a treat is a good way to get your puppy acquainted with the idea before you ask them to find a toy.

- Start small by asking your dog to stay while you set the toy within sight.
- Tell your dog to go and get the toys as you would if you were playing a regular game of fetch.
- Build complexity for your puppy by asking them to stay while you hide the toy in different places around the house.

Your puppy will have a lot of fun searching out their toy. This is a great way to occupy your dog and use up their mind without having to be very active yourself.

Similarly, you can purchase puzzle toys for your dog. With a puzzle toy, you hide small treats within the toy hidden behind closed doors. Your dog will have to remove, slide, or adjust the trap doors to reveal the prize. Micah loves playing with puzzle toys. They are especially good for keeping your dog mentally active while you are out of the house. Before I leave the house for an extended period of time, I always fill up a puzzle toy with treats and let Micah play with it while I'm gone.

Fetch and find

This is another great game to build your puppy's self-control and satisfy instincts. It works best when your puppy is already very acquainted with fetch. Ask your puppy to sit and stay and then toss a toy out of sight. Release your dog to go look for the toy. Teach your puppy to follow your commands for left or right, forward or back, to help them find the toy.

This game helps your puppy to learn to look to you when they're looking for something. It can help them to overcome the desire to chase things inappropriately later on.

How to teach your puppy not to chase

Many Maltese puppies will want to chase things that they shouldn't as they get older. The best way to train your puppy not to chase things they shouldn't is to offer plenty of positive chasing and searching games that encourage self-control, like the ones mentioned above. However, even if you engage your dog in lots of positive activities, they'll still feel the drive to chase something that they shouldn't at times.

For this reason, it is essential always to keep your Maltese puppy on a leash if you are not in a fenced area until they are mentally mature enough to practice self-control in these environments. A long line attached to your Maltese harness is a great way to control and train while also giving the dog opportunities to practice self-control. Just be careful that the long line never stops your puppy abruptly, as this can damage their back even if they are on a harness.

Micah has mastered this technique. He sticks right by our side when on walks and very rarely attempts to chase anything. On a rare occasion, he will try to chase a squirrel or a bird. Micah is so good at staying by our side that we occasionally walk him around the neighborhood without a leash, although this is not advised and is certainly a bad habit.

Photo Courtesy of Regina Kapsiotis

Housetraining

"Patience, consistency, and persistence during the first few weeks will bring quick and lasting rewards. Their heart's desire is to please you. Praise for a job well done will go a long way in keeping your puppy motivated to do as you ask."

BARBARA SHEWMAKE
Storybook Maltese

Like most toy breeds, Maltese are not especially well-known for being easy to house train. While they are not as challenging as some breeds, most do require a little bit of time to be fully housetrained. You may find that your dog is prone to accidents fairly long into their puppyhood, especially if the weather is poor. Maltese are known for not liking to go outside in inclement weather to do their business.

Micah was difficult to potty train at first, and I understand that it can be frustrating. Nowadays, he never has an accident in the house. Micah can be left home alone for upwards of six hours without having a single accident. Don't give up!

Here are some tips for successfully potty training your Maltese:

Supervision

Like so many other aspects of raising your Maltese, supervision is key in potty training. Every time that you miss your puppy having an accident, you reinforce your puppy's tendency to go to the bathroom inside. You also miss an opportunity to reinforce that your puppy should go outside.

Reprimanding or punishing your puppy after the fact will only confuse your puppy. For sensitive breeds like the Maltese, being reprimanded or punished for reasons they do not understand can have severe consequences. Maltese that are punished for potty training accidents that they don't understand often become nervous dogs. Be patient but vigilant in your training.

Paper training

Many Maltese are more successfully trained when they learn to go potty inside on paper, otherwise known as "puppy pads," at least at first. Your Maltese won't have an aversion to going on the paper like they might have

to going outside when the weather isn't good. It is very easy to redirect your dog to the paper when you think that they are posturing to go.

Maltese puppies have very small bladders but very big senses of adventure. By the time your Maltese pauses in their play to realize that they have to go to the bathroom, they may not be able to hold it for very long.

Paper training allows your Maltese to know exactly where they can go and allows them to go quickly without having to get your attention to go outside. If you live in an apartment, especially on a higher story, paper training may be even more effective.

Although we didn't use paper training techniques for Micah, we use paper training for many of the dogs that we foster. It's incredibly effective when you don't have time to constantly supervise. Be aware that paper training should only be used as an alternative to taking your dog outside when you don't have the time. Allowing your dog to get too comfortable with paper training is a bad thing and may lead your dog to believe that pottying inside is allowable.

"Here's a tip: If you have a potty pad then add newspaper on it. People forget at times to watch the puppy all the time and any house rug or carpet will become a potty pad easily. The newspaper makes a wrinkle noise that helps them identify that it is the potty spot."

SHASTA GRIMES
Desert Hobby Ranch

Potty training your Maltese

1 COMMAND FOR POTTY

Whether you want to train your puppy to go inside on a pad or outdoors, the first step will be teaching your puppy a command for going potty. When your puppy goes, say the command and give your puppy a reward. When you take your puppy out to go potty first thing in the morning, and you know that they're about to go, use the command word and then reward your dog when they go.

Soon, your Maltese will understand the command for go potty. This is very useful because you can get ahead of your dog's potty schedule and ask them to go outside and go potty even if they don't realize they need to go.

2 SCHEDULE AND ANTICIPATE

If your puppy gets a food toy or a bowl with their breakfast every morning at about the same time, you can expect them to need to relieve themselves at a predictable time after this. Take your puppy out and ask them to go potty when you expect them to need to go, rather than waiting for them to need to go and ask you. The more you can anticipate your puppy's needs and get ahead of them, the more you will affirm that they are supposed to go on the paper or outside.

As a puppy, Micah had to relieve himself once every thirty minutes. Water and food move through Maltese puppies particularly fast because of their small stature. I set a timer for 30 minutes as a reminder to take Micah outside. Getting in a routine like that is healthy not only for your puppy but also for yourself.

3 SUPERVISE AND RESPOND

Always watch your puppy when they aren't in their crate and redirect them if they try to go to the bathroom inappropriately. Do not be harsh, but firmly tell your puppy "no" and show them where you do want them to go, rewarding them enthusiastically for going in the appropriate place.

There is no point in reprimanding your puppy after the fact. They will not associate having gone to the bathroom with your reprimand. If you can't supervise your puppy, they should be in a crate small enough that they do not feel comfortable going potty in it. Remember that your puppy will not necessarily feel the same instinct on your couch or bed, which is big enough for them to get away from their sleeping area to do business.

The fear stages

All dogs, regardless of the breed, go through two fear stages. During these stages, you'll see some behavior changes. Dogs are more sensitive to frightening, painful, or traumatic experiences during this time.

Photo Courtesy of Crystal Jones

Traumatic experiences for your dog during this period, even if you don't notice them, can have lasting effects. Dogs' brains are more sensitive to negative experiences during this time and more likely to form lasting connotations because of them.

First fear stage

The first fear stage is right when you are usually getting your puppy, between 8 and 10 weeks of age. You are unlikely to notice this period because it will coincide with the time when you are getting your puppy. Your puppy will seem cautious of new things and people in their environments, but this will seem normal, considering your puppy is just settling into your home.

For Maltese, it may be a bit more dangerous when they come out of the first fear stage. At about ten weeks, your Maltese puppy may suddenly seem to have a burst of confidence and get into things they shouldn't without the least bit of anxiety. Be on the lookout for this sudden burst of confidence as your puppy nears ten weeks.

Second fear stage

The second fear period comes in adolescence, when your puppy is between 6 and 14 months of age. During this time, your puppy will have developed more independence and be mastering some basic obedience, so it can come as a real surprise when your puppy suddenly starts showing fear of new things.

FUN FACT
Trainability

Maltese have a reputation for being slightly stubborn and occasionally vocal, but their desire for human affection and intelligence makes them quick learners. Overall, Maltese make excellent companion dogs, but proper socialization and training are essential in raising a well-adjusted companion dog. Therefore, the first three months are the optimal time to introduce your Maltese to various experiences, including sounds, environments, and people.

Your Maltese may suddenly be afraid of strangers or new dogs or even novel stimuli in the environment like a statue or flag. They may suddenly seem to be aware of things that they didn't think were dangerous before, like going over a small bridge or near a busy road.

Micah became deathly afraid of the vacuum. When he was a puppy, he loved chasing around the vacuum and biting it. Around 6 to 14 months of age, Micah became terrified of the loud sound coming from the vacuum. In fact, he tried to hide and leave the room immediately whenever the vacuum was turned on. He was similarly afraid of cars and bicycles on the road. He was intimidated by their large size and loud noise so much so that he wanted to be picked up and held when they passed by.

What to do during the fear periods

During both fear periods, it is essential that you protect your Maltese from negative experiences. Negative interactions with other dogs during this time can be especially harmful, leaving your Maltese scared of other dogs. A simple incident like a nail trimmed too short may leave your puppy petrified of nail trims for life.

It is important to protect your Maltese from negative experiences throughout their development. Still, during most of your dog's puppyhood, you will play a balance between giving your puppy new experiences, socialization, exposure, and protecting them from danger. During the fear periods, it is more important to protect your puppy from a negative experience than it is for them to get ongoing socialization or new experiences.

Entertainment for eager minds

Maltese are clever little dogs who are always learning, whether you are actively teaching them or not. As you raise your Maltese, you will want to provide plenty of stimulation and engagement for their active minds. Such entertainment is important for you to raise a healthy and engaged dog, but it is also important to protect your home from a Maltese's destructiveness. Here are some ways to keep your Maltese entertained:

- **BUILD A HEALTHY OBSESSION WITH TOYS.** Maltese are not as naturally toy-obsessed as some other breeds like retrievers, but most Maltese learn to love their toys with proper encouragement from their owners. Encourage your Maltese to play with toys by themselves from an early age so they'll be able to keep themselves busy when you don't have time.
- **USE PUZZLE GAMES.** Use food distributing toys, stuff smaller toys into larger pockets for your dog to pull out, and use toys that challenge your dog in other ways. Such toys are great ways to entertain your dog and build physical intelligence.
- **SELF-CONTROL TRAINING.** One of the things that will require the most mental dedication for your puppy is learning how to stay still and focus on you. Simply teaching your puppy to stay for longer periods, even while you do other things, is an amazing way to occupy their mind.
- **PLAY DATES.** Most Maltese love playing with other dogs, especially small dogs who are well-matched to them in size and energy level. If you don't have another dog, consider setting up a play date so that your Maltese can have some socialization.

CHAPTER 8

Things to Do With Your Maltese

"A Maltese can get an adequate amount of exercise just playing in the house, but they enjoy a nice walk or romp in the back yard. As long as their exercise is shared with their new parent or family, they will be happy."

KAREN ORSIN
Petite Pups

Photo Courtesy of Katherine Learned

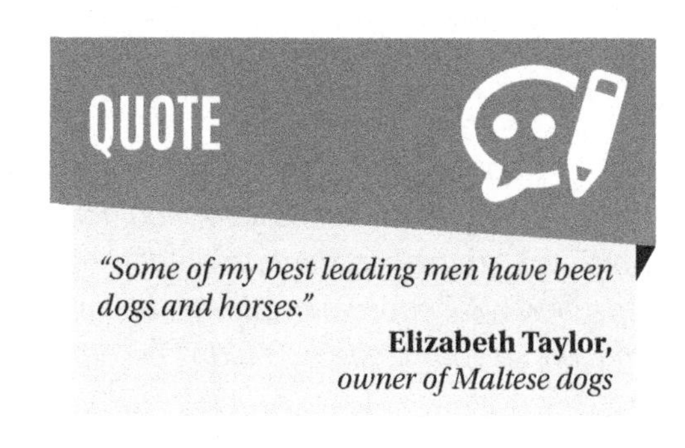

Maltese are excellent companions, and you will surely enjoy just hanging out with your loving, adorable dog. However, there are lots of things that you can do with your Maltese. These clever dogs excel in a range of disciplines. Most are happy to learn and love pleasing you. Here are some things you can enjoy doing with your Maltese.

Obedience

Maltese are smart and love to learn. Most have a lot of fun learning new tricks and seem to enjoy going through their trick repertoire. Most Maltese tend to be a little bit better at competitive obedience and trick training than they are at learning to modify behavior. This is to say that they are wonderful at obeying when they want to obey.

Luckily for you, if you want to train your Maltese in competitive obedience, one of the places most Maltese are most happy to obey is in front of a crowd. This is not a dog to leave you looking like a fool when you ask for a command in front of your friends. Maltese seem to take joy in putting on a show and impressing a crowd.

You are likely to find that your Maltese excels in complex structured obedience. As an added benefit, you can astound strangers for the next 15 years about how well-trained your "puppy" is since most people mistake Maltese for puppies long into their lives.

Agility

Many people are surprised by just how agile Maltese are. Although these dogs are very small, they are perfectly proportioned and quite athletic. A Maltese in full coat looks truly beautiful flying over the jumps in an agility competition.

Maltese tend to remain focused on their handler, even when they are active, which makes them well-suited to agility. Agility is a great activity for Maltese because it will teach them to focus on you, have confidence, and because it is a lot of fun for your dog. Because Maltese are so small, you can easily set up a home agility course to train them or just for your own fun.

Trick training

"Positive behavior is likely to be repeated if it is positively reinforced. While training your Maltese, you should use plenty of encouragement and treats, which will strengthen the human-dog bond. Consistent training methods and repetition will shape your puppy's behavior. Training sessions should be short and fun, so your Maltese wouldn't become bored."

LEONA LUPULESKU
Leona's Maltese

Photo Courtesy of Gabriele Puplauskaite

The Maltese Dog, released in 2015, chronicles the dog-napping of a celebrity dog named Skipper the Maltese. FBI agents Fong and Wong lead the search when Skipper goes missing.

One of the things that Maltese are best at is tricks. Your Maltese really doesn't know the difference between standard obedience training and trick training. They just know that they should be focused on you and learn to do whatever you're asking. Trick training is a great way to break up your standard obedience training. Besides, it's a fun thing to show off to your friends. The eager and playful Maltese can learn all kinds of adorable tricks that your friends and family will love. Here are just a few ideas to get you started.

- **DANCE.** Your Maltese spins in a circle continuously or one loop at a time.
- **STAND UP.** Your Maltese stands up on their hind legs. This command can also be conjoined with "Dance" to teach your dog to stand up while dancing.
- **PLAY DEAD.** Your Maltese rolls over on their back and perhaps covers their face on command.
- **SHAKE OR HIGH FIVE.** Your Maltese gives you their paw on command, either reaching out or jumping up to hit your hand with their paw.
- **ROLL OVER.** Your Maltese rolls all the way over. This command can be challenging unless your dog is on carpet or something else that is easy to grip.
- **COVER YOUR FACE.** Your Maltese reaches up to put their paws over their nose or face.
- **CRAWL.** Your Maltese crouches down and crawls. It is cute combined with "cover your face" to make a joke about your dog being ashamed about something.
- **SPEAK.** This isn't just a fun command. Teaching your dog how to bark on command is a good way to teach them how to also stop barking on command.

Don't feel like you have to stick to one trick at a time. Maltese are very clever and have good memories, so they can learn how to do a series of commands to make a fun routine. In fact, many Maltese learn a routine easier than individual tricks separately.

Photo Courtesy of HeatherAnn Goodrich

You can also teach your Maltese hand commands for their tricks so that you can ask them to go through a routine without anyone being able to tell that you are even giving the commands.

Therapy

Maltese excel as therapy dogs. Because they are so outgoing, loving, and empathetic to humans, they seem to naturally sense what people might need. As a therapy dog, your Maltese may be able to understand when a patient would be cheered by a playful show or game of fetch or when a person would rather just have the dog lie quietly on the bed with them.

As long as your Maltese gets good socialization growing up, they are likely to be very well suited to work as a therapy dog. Because they're small, clean, and hypoallergenic, the breed is favored in hospitals as well. Very few people will be scared of or intimidated by a Maltese, so they are a good fit for even a children's hospital.

I can vouch that Maltese are excellent therapy dogs. I purchased Micah several months after my father passed away. Micah helped comfort me and fill a hole of sorrow and sadness. Micah's kindness and gentle nature helped me when I needed it most.

Emotional support

For the same reason that Maltese make good therapy dogs, they can make excellent emotional support dogs. It is important to keep in mind that while Maltese favor their own family, they tend to be outgoing and loving towards everyone they meet. For some people, this is a downside in an emotional support dog because you may prefer your dog to be focused only on you. Keep this in mind if you are choosing a Maltese for your emotional support dog. Otherwise, Maltese fit the role of emotional support dog extremely well.

Micah works as an emotional support animal for my fiancé. She suffers from anxiety in public places such as airplanes. Her doctor wrote a note for Micah so that he is a certified emotional support animal. Micah almost instinctually knows when my fiancé is suffering from an anxiety attack. He cuddles and kisses her until she calms down and helps keep her distracted from her anxiety attacks.

Photo Courtesy of Myra Yu Abamonga

Service

Maltese can excel in certain types of service work. Their small size prevents them from being very useful in a physical sense, but they can be ideal for seizure alert dogs, hearing alert dogs, and in a variety of other roles. Their small size and hypoallergenic hair make them convenient to take everywhere as service dogs.

Because they can easily fit in a bag, it's no trouble to bring them along with you no matter where you go. Although Maltese may not be quite as sensitive and emotionally tuned to their owners as some breeds, they have an outgoing nature which makes them well-suited to going with their owner everywhere in a busy life.

Photo Courtesy of Stephanie Agostino

Full-time companion

Perhaps the best job for any Maltese, regardless of what other role they play, is as a full-time companion. Maltese love their families and are gregarious and bold enough to go anywhere with their people. These are the ideal dogs for boats, RVs, apartment living, and anywhere where there is a small space.

These conveniently sized pups can fit into a bag where they may be allowed into more businesses than other dogs would be. You may be able to take your Maltese nearly everywhere with you, which couldn't make them happier.

CHAPTER 9
Grooming

Maltese are coveted as prized show dogs thanks to their head-to-toe mantle of long, silky white hair. Even though their fur is single-coated, and they don't shed, grooming challenges still present themselves. Keeping their hair clean, white, and mat-free requires regular maintenance. As a Maltese owner, you'll have to keep up with brushing, bathing, working out mats, and battling tearstains.

When it comes to grooming, you'll have to ask yourself some very important questions: Should I do it myself or go to a professional? Do I want a puppy cut or a long cut? Should the groomer use clippers or scissors? How often do I trim my dog's nails? How do I get rid of mats?

Photo Courtesy of Leona Lupulesku Leona's Maltese

Do it yourself or go to a professional?

Whether you should cut your dog's hair yourself or pay a professional to do it boils down to your expectations. If you're going for a showroom look, then you're better off paying a professional. If you're looking to save some money, then grooming your dog at home is the better option. Whichever route you decide to go, maintaining your Maltese's coat is an ongoing effort that should be done with care.

If you can't dedicate the time to learn or the money to invest in good equipment, then you'd be better off taking your dog to a groomer. Grooming your dog at home is costly up-front but can save money in the long run. Dog clippers can run anywhere from $30 all the way up to $150 and beyond. It's best to invest in a more expensive pair of clippers up-front as cheap clippers can burn out quickly and overheat, which causes clipper burn.

Cutting your dog's hair at home takes time, patience, and practice. There are many great tutorials on YouTube to help you learn, but you're still likely to go through some trial and error. Be prepared to set aside two to three hours to properly groom your dog. This includes bathing, nail clipping, brushing out mats, and actually cutting your dog's hair. Rushing through grooming won't only result in a bad haircut but may also end up hurting your pet.

Regardless of if you choose to groom your dog at home or use a professional, you should be grooming your Maltese once every six weeks at a minimum. If you plan on using your Maltese as a show dog, then you'll need to get your pet groomed once per month. You should expect to pay anywhere from $30 to $90 to get your dog professionally groomed. Over the course of a year, that will add up to $260 to $780 per year.

Much like with the clippers, you get what you pay for. Paying for the cheapest groomer possible may be an unpleasant experience for your dog that results in clipper burn, choppy haircuts, and overall trauma. Cheap groomers likely use cheap equipment and have less training and experience than more expensive groomers. Be sure to do your research and read customer reviews before taking your dog to a new groomer.

Professional dog groomers include a multitude of services for your Maltese. Most of the time, you'll be looking for a "full service" deal that includes a haircut, nail trim, and bath. Other add-ons include teeth brushing, breath refreshing, ear cleaning, anal gland expression, flea and tick treatment, facials, paw balm, and even nail polish.

Photo Courtesy of Ugnė Petrovaitė

Questions to ask the groomer

It's important to make your expectations clear with the groomer. There may be some trial and error until your groomer learns exactly how you like your dog's haircut. Below is a list of topics to cover:

- How long do you want your dog's hair (puppy cut or long cut)?
- Do you want the face square or rounded?
- Should the groomer use clippers or scissors?
- Does your Maltese have any allergies or sensitivities to shampoos?
- Is there anywhere that the dog doesn't like to be touched?
- Are there any mats to be aware of?
- Are there any areas to focus on (tearstains)?
- Do you have experience with Maltese?

We give our groomer a heads-up that Micah is susceptible to matting in his armpits and behind his ears. This way, the groomer focuses on those areas. We also have the groomer focus on Micah's eyes since he deals with staining. Micah has sensitive skin, so we request a special oat milk shampoo be used. His sensitive skin also means that we can only scissor cut him as clippers irritate his skin. Lastly, Micah doesn't like getting his butt touched. It's important to relay any information like this to groomers so that they don't get bitten by accident.

Long coat or puppy cut?

"Whether growing your Maltese out or keeping him in a 'puppy cut', combing through the coat daily is essential to avoid mats. It doesn't take long (if done daily) and can be a bonding experience for you and your dog. Teach the puppy to lie on his back and let you gently comb through the hair on his legs and belly. Next comb the back, sides, front, and rear of your puppy, finishing off with the face."

BARBARA SHEWMAKE
Storybook Maltese

There is not a more head-turning breed of dog in the world than a Maltese with a long coat. Conversely, it's hard to find a dog as adorable as a Maltese with a puppy cut. Whether you want a long coat or a puppy cut boils down to your expectations and the amount of time that you invest in your dog's good looks.

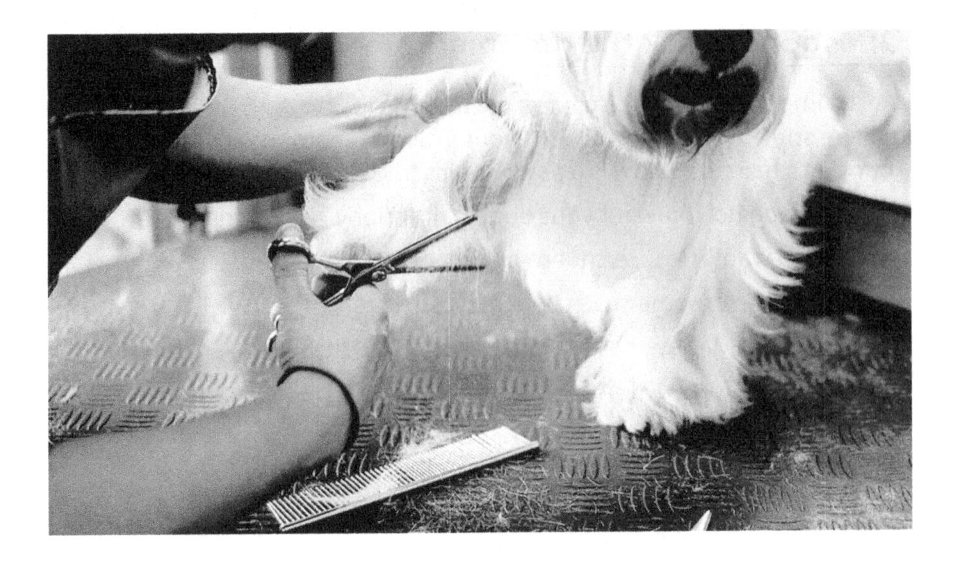

Long coat

A long coat, otherwise known as a show coat, will certainly put your dog in the spotlight. As attractive as a long coat on a Maltese is, it takes a ton of work to maintain. To maintain a long coat, you must be prepared to establish a nightly grooming schedule that includes brushing, mat removal, and tearstain maintenance. Keeping your dog's hair long needs to become a hobby that you enjoy; otherwise, it will become laborious.

Keeping your Maltese's coat long and healthy is a positive way to bond with your pup. Pampering your dog's majestic hair while brushing it can become enjoyable for both of you. Beware that if you don't have the time or patience to maintain this long hair though, it can backfire. Long hair can quickly turn into painful mats. Long hair that once symbolized beauty can quickly turn to symbolize neglect.

Long hair on your Maltese will allow you to accessorize, unlike short hair. You can use bows and clips and even give it a little ponytail. The possibilities are endless.

Puppy cut

Maltese are one of the few breeds of dogs that can maintain a puppy-like appearance throughout their entire life. This is thanks to the puppy cut. The puppy cut is a short haircut that is typically accomplished with clippers. It prevents your dog from developing painful mats and allows your Maltese to cool down during the hot summer months.

Beware that cutting your Maltese's hair too short can cause discomfort. Maltese are not meant to have buzzed hair. In fact, their skin is too sensitive to have short hair as it doesn't have enough melanin to protect it from the sunlight. A Maltese always needs at least a quarter-inch of hair or more to protect it from harmful UV rays. A Maltese's hair also protects it from the cold. It's wise to keep your pet's hair on the long side during the winter and on the short side during the summer.

The puppy cut may not be as versatile as a show cut, but there are still some choices that you can make to have your dog stand out. You can choose to have a rounded face or a square face. A rounded face gives the dog a teddy bear appearance, whereas a square face gives your dog a Shih Tzu appearance. Many Maltese owners choose to leave a bushy face and tail while trimming the body short.

We like to keep Micah's hair short all around. We request a puppy cut with a rounded, teddy bear face. Micah mats very quickly, and it is much less of a hassle to keep his hair short rather than constantly battle mats. Not only are mats frustrating to get out, but they can also itch and cause pain. If we let Micah's hair get too long, then he can get his nails stuck in his mats while trying to scratch himself, which causes him to yip in pain.

Having fun with cuts

The versatility of the Maltese's majestic coat allows you to cut it and style it in ways that other breeds can only dream of. Below is a list of haircut ideas and hairstyles to have fun with:

- **SHOW CUT:** A long and silky appearance where the hair is maintained at a length that just barely touches the ground.
- **PUPPY CUT:** Between one-quarter inch and one inch all around. It's easy to maintain and keeps your dog looking youthful throughout its entire life.
- **TEDDY BEAR CUT:** The body is clipped to one-quarter inch, whereas everywhere else is left long. The face is then rounded and fluffed up to give it that big-headed teddy bear look that we all know and love.
- **BOB CUT:** By leaving the ears and mustache long, a Maltese can achieve the same bob haircut that humans have.
- **KOREAN FACE:** A popular style for Maltese in Korea, this haircut gives a doll-faced appearance. It consists of a very short chin, a medium-length mustache, and very long ears.
- **GROOMED EARS:** If you let your Maltese's ears grow long and keep the rest of the body short, then you can curl, add bows, or even perm your dog's ear hair. Be careful as Maltese's ears are delicate and easy to damage.
- **BRAIDS:** The long and silky hair of the Maltese is easy to put into braids. Braids look the best on top of the head or at their ears.
- **FLARED FEET:** Much like flared jeans of the 1970s, you can intentionally leave your dog's leg hair long and flush it outwards with a brush to give it that same look.
- **TOP KNOT:** A top knot can be achieved with just about any hair length. This helps keep hair out of your dog's eyes and looks adorable. Just make sure to not pull too tightly, or it can cause your Maltese discomfort.
- **BOWS:** A gentleman pup can sport a bowtie, while a lady can tie a cute bow into her hair.

Micah doesn't seem to enjoy having his hair up in a top knot and doesn't like wearing accessories like bows and hair clips. Since we choose to keep his hair short, we haven't gotten to experiment with too many hairstyles.

Scissor cutting tips

Cutting your Maltese's hair at home can be intimidating at first. Follow the tips below one step at a time to achieve a consistent haircut that looks just like the professionals did it:

- **PURCHASE A HIGH-QUALITY SET OF GROOMING SCISSORS:** A cheap set of scissors will be less sharp and more difficult to cut with. Look for a full set of grooming scissors with grooming shears, curved scissors for rounding, thinning shears, and safety-tip scissors for delicate areas near the eyes and tail.
- **PREPARE YOUR EQUIPMENT:** Before you make your first cut, make sure that your scissors are cleaned, sharpened, and oiled. Dull scissor blades will pull on your pet's hair rather than cutting it. Adding a few drops of scissor oil on a sharp pair of blades will help you effortlessly cut your dog's hair.
- **SET UP A GROOMING STATION:** Make sure that your grooming station is located on a hard surface where hair is easy to clean up. Your little Maltese should also be elevated so that you have a good angle and vision and don't need to reach.
- **GIVE YOUR MALTESE A BATH:** Much like at the hair salon, it's easiest to cut your dog's hair when it is wet. Give your Maltese a bath and dry its hair off so that it is not dripping wet. This minimizes your dog's curls and allows you to get a more even cut.
- **COMB OUT YOUR MALTESE'S HAIR:** If your Maltese is badly matted, then you should brush out the mats prior to getting the dog's hair wet. Otherwise, it's okay to brush your Maltese's hair after its bath since the hair will be easier to work with. Brush your Maltese from the top of its head down to its tail, going with the direction of the fur.
- **TOP OF THE HEAD:** Start at the top of the head and trim to any length that you desire. Use a short blade with safety tips. Be sure to comb and cut away from the eyes.
- **TIPS OF THE EARS:** Put your fingers at the end of your Maltese's ears to avoid cutting them. You can either cut a straight line or follow the curve of the ear, depending on personal preference. Be sure to trim underneath the ears as well.
- **BODY (FRONT TO BACK):** Using a pair of straight shears, start at the top of your Maltese's neck and cut in straight lines all the way down to its tail. Don't cut the tail quite yet. Continue cutting this way until the entire back and sides of your Maltese are trimmed to your liking.

- **NECK AND CHEST:** It's easiest to trim the neck and chest after they are freshly brushed. Trim off the excess hair and continue down to the chest. It looks best if you blend the length of the neck and chest together. Use thinning shears for any thick areas that are susceptible to mats. Be sure to hold the scissors parallel to the body while cutting and use a comb to help blend in between cuts.
- **LEGS:** Begin from the bottom up by trimming the feathers along the back of the leg. Continue up your Maltese's legs and repeat in the front. Make sure to trim between your Maltese's toes and remember to trim the hair that grows between the paw pads as well.
- **TAIL:** Brush the hair out and allow the hair to hang down. Grab the hair and pull it straight out, and cut a straight line or curved line to any length that you please. Brush the hair out once more and trim any stray fur.
- **ANUS:** Cut the anus area very short. This prevents any feces from getting stuck on your dog's fur, which is common in Maltese.
- **BRUSH OUT, AND SPOT CHECK:** Once finished, brush your Maltese out one last time, cut away stray hairs, and blend unevenness.

Clipper cutting tips

Clipper cutting is quicker and easier than cutting with scissors. There are different steps that you should be aware of that are highlighted below:

1. **PURCHASE HIGH-QUALITY CLIPPERS:** High-quality clippers are not only more efficient at cutting, but they are also quieter and stay cooler. Loud noises like vacuums or thunderstorms can easily scare your Maltese. Clippers are no different. More expensive clippers tend to be quieter and less intimidating for your pup. High-quality clippers come with sharper blades and tend to last longer. They also don't overheat as quickly, which can cause clipper burn and irritation.
2. **PREPARE YOUR EQUIPMENT:** Make sure that your blades are sharp for an effortless cut. Clipper blades can be affordably replaced if they get too dull. Spray on a clipper coolant or lubricant to prevent clipper burn. It's recommended that you keep a spare clipper blade nearby in case the first one starts to overheat.
3. **SET UP A GROOMING STATION:** Make sure that your grooming station is located on a hard surface where hair is easy to clean up. Your little Maltese should also be elevated so that you have a good angle and vision and don't need to reach.

4. **GIVE YOUR MALTESE A BATH:** Unlike with scissor cutting, you'll want your Maltese's hair to completely dry out after its bath. This is because clippers can get stuck and tangled on wet and heavy hair. You can either let your Maltese's hair air dry, or you can blow dry it.

5. **CUT OUT MATS:** Locate your Maltese's existing mats and brush them out. If you're unable to brush them out, then just cut them out at the base. Clippers may get tangled in your dog's mats and cause them pain, so it's important to eliminate them before you start.

> **HELPFUL TIP**
> **Avoiding A Dried Out Coat**
>
> 
>
> One of the Maltese's signature features is their silky, white coat. Maintaining luxurious locks is an essential part of your Maltese's grooming routine, but what do you do when your Maltese's coat is too dry? Too frequent bathing is a common factor in drying out a Maltese's coat, as well as using too harsh shampoos that strip important oils from the hair. Over and under-brushing can also cause your dog's coat to become dry and brittle. Bathing should typically be done every four to six weeks and brushing several times per week. Leave-in conditioning sprays and softening sprays can also be administered.

6. **CHOOSE YOUR BLADE LENGTH:** You should have a set of guards handy that help you achieve the length of cut that you're looking for.

7. **GO IN THE RIGHT DIRECTION:** It's time to start cutting your Maltese's hair. Make sure that you go in the same direction that the hair grows. Pay close attention to which way your Maltese's hair is growing so that the cut is smooth and even.

8. **FACE AND TAIL:** The face and tail should always be cut with scissors. Take extreme care and use shortened safety-tipped scissors for these areas.

TIP: Frequently check the temperature of your clippers while cutting. Excessive heat can cause clipper burn, which may take weeks to heal. If your clipper blade gets too hot, then switch it out for a spare and continue. If you don't have a spare, then you should put the blade down until it cools off. Try putting it on a baking sheet or another piece of metal, as it will quickly transfer the heat and cool your blade down.

Getting rid of mats

Maltese are particularly susceptible to matting, thanks to their long silky coat. Mats are caused when hair is rubbed together, which causes tangling. The most common spots that mats occur in are behind the ears, between the legs, under the chest, and on the tail. Collars may also cause matting around the neck. If left unattended, new fur can grow into matted fur, making the problem even worse.

Mats continue to grow and tighten closer and closer to the skin. The tightness of mats causes a pinching and hair-pulling sensation that can upset your Maltese. Extreme matting can damage your dog's skin as it prevents moisture from reaching the skin and can weaken the hair follicles. If your Maltese is active like Micah, then he is even more susceptible to mats because of the additional movement.

Preventing mats by frequently brushing your dog is ideal. If you see a mat forming, then you should either use a brush or comb to work it out. Identifying mats early and brushing them out as soon as they begin forming is best. Mats become much more difficult to brush out once they become larger and tighter.

Try gently working the mat apart with your fingertips while combing out smaller tangles. Keep a close eye on your dog's skin while separating mats, and avoid pulling the hair if possible. Hold the hair below the tangle with a tight grip to prevent painful hair pulling. Oil-based detangling sprays will help with tough mats. It's important to move slowly and be patient to avoid hurting your Maltese.

If you've tried detangling oil, separating with your fingers, brushing the mat, and it still won't come out, then you may need to cut the mat out. Cut the mat at its base with a short safety-tipped pair of scissors. Be careful not to accidentally cut your Maltese's skin.

I intentionally keep Micah's hair short in areas where he is susceptible to matting. Since Micah is such an active dog, we keep his hair short under his armpits, behind his ear, and at the base of his tail. Micah lets us know when he has a mat as he is constantly scratching and biting at it. As soon as we notice a mat on Micah, we cut it out immediately.

Nails

Nail trimming is essential in dog grooming but can be difficult, especially for anxiety-laden pets. It's easiest to trim your dog's nails with the help of another person. One person does the cutting while the other distracts with treats or toys. If your dog despises having its feet touched, then you may need to restrain it. It's mentally tough to have to physically restrain your dog, but trimming its nails is essential for good health and hygiene.

Having trouble cutting your dog's nails? Many dog owners claim that a little peanut butter on a spoon works like magic. Your dog will be distracted licking the peanut butter off a spoon while you carefully cut its nails.

Much like with clippers and scissors, it's important to choose the right equipment. You can use either a set of nail clippers or nail grinders. Nail grinders make a noise similar to hair clippers and may be intimidating to your dog. Nail grinders are nice because they dull out your dog's nails, whereas nail clippers can unintentionally make them sharper. Nail grinders are sold with either grinding stones or finishing stones. Grinding stones are ideal for trimming the nail, whereas finishing stones are ideal for buffing and smoothing the nail out. Most nail clippers come with built-in safety guards to prevent accidentally poking your Maltese.

How to cut your Maltese's nails

If you have never cut your Maltese's nails before, then you may want to take your pet to a professional groomer or veterinarian to teach you how.

Start slowly by picking up your Maltese's paw firmly. If your dog is anxious, then try to distract it with a treat or a toy while cutting its nails. I prefer to cut Micah's nails while he is on my lap. That way, he is more comfortable and less anxious. It's wise to cut back the fur between your Maltese's toenails before trimming.

Gently but firmly squeeze the paw pad so that the nails extend outwards into a claw. This gives you the best vision and angle at cutting your Maltese's nails. Start from the outside of the paw inwards by clipping the tip of the nail straight across. Avoid clipping beyond the curve of the nail, or else you may accidentally cut a blood vessel. You should easily be able to tell where this blood vessel is in a Maltese. Just look for a chalky white ring in the center of the nail and avoid cutting there at all costs.

Don't panic if you accidentally cut the blood vessel. Just apply gentle pressure until it clots and clean up the blood afterward. If you cannot stop the bleeding or it seems excessive, then take your Maltese to the vet as soon as possible.

In rare cases, your Maltese will despise nail trimming so much that it has to be done professionally by a veterinarian. Maltese very rarely have to be sedated for nail trimming, although it is a possibility.

Photo Courtesy of Austin Parsons

Tooth brushing

Brushing your dog's teeth will help prevent periodontal diseases like gingivitis and tooth decay. Much like humans, a Maltese's teeth should be brushed to prevent plaque buildup and bad breath. It's advised to train your dog to accept tooth brushing at a young age and to make it a habit.

Your local pet store should sell toothbrushes that are specifically designed for dogs. You'll need to find a small toothbrush that is designed for small breeds. These special toothbrushes include angled handles, multiple heads, and even finger toothbrushes. It's also acceptable to use toothbrushes that are designed for babies.

Human toothpaste should be avoided as it can cause an upset stomach. Human toothpaste consists of xylitol which may be toxic for dogs. It also contains high levels of sodium which is unsafe for your Maltese. Baking soda should also be avoided as it is highly alkaline and can damage your dog's digestive tract.

Pet toothpaste is uniquely flavored so that it is appetizing for your Maltese. Flavors include beef, poultry, and fish. A flavor that tastes good to your Maltese will result in a more pleasant experience for both of you.

To brush your Maltese's teeth, start with the lower teeth by gently tilting your dog's head upwards. Focus first on the large cheek teeth as well as the canine teeth. These two areas are where plaque accumulates the quickest. Most periodontal damage occurs to the outer surfaces of your dog's teeth, so don't panic if your pup doesn't allow you to brush the inner surfaces. Brush each side for approximately 30 seconds.

CHAPTER 10
Socialization

"Socializing means taking the puppy to various environments four times a week and having the puppy interact with different types of people and pets as often as possible. This is essential for the puppy to thrive and develop properly. The puppy should be treated as a part of the family. Remember that the puppy is what you make him/her, the environment and how the puppy is raised plays a critical role in how your puppy will turn out."

LEONA LUPULESKU
Leona's Maltese

Photo Courtesy of Katherine Learned

Maltese love companionship, and it's advisable to socialize them with other humans and animals starting out at a young age. Dogs and other pets are territorial by nature, so it may be difficult to introduce them to other pets if they aren't used to interactions with other animals. Socializing your Maltese with other animals not only will keep him in good physical shape but is also mentally stimulating and will help it lead a happier life.

FUN FACT
Cinnamon

The 2011 film *Cinnamon* follows the adventures of a pampered Maltese who is in for a rude awakening when her owner, Madeline, meets the love of her life, Kevin. Cinnamon and a team of her canine companions band together in an attempt to break Madeline and Kevin up. Will she succeed, or will she realize that having a family is better than the alternative? Watch the film to find out!

Protect your dog

"It is said that the Maltese has the heart of a lion. This is because a Maltese doesn't know he's an adorable little powder puff. In his heart, he is the 'King of the Jungle'. He is fearless! This can lead to trouble if he encounters another animal big enough to cause him harm."

BARBARA SHEWMAKE
Storybook Maltese

It's important to understand your Maltese's mannerisms before introducing them to a new person or pet. There is a distinct difference between a playful bark and an angry bark. The same goes for a playful whimper and a painful whimper. You can tell a lot about how your dog is feeling about a situation based on their body language and vocals.

First and foremost, it's important to keep your Maltese safe when introducing them to new animals. For example, if you're introducing your new Maltese to your friend's new dog, it is important to have an up-front conversation with your friend about its behavior. Has it had any altercations with other dogs? Is it playful? Is it well-trained? Learning about your friend's dog's behavior will help you assess the situation so you can break the dogs up before their interaction turns to aggression.

Keeping your dog on a harness with a leash attached is also helpful. Make sure that you aren't actively restraining the dog as it can cause tension. Let your Maltese sniff around and interact with the other animal while checking to make sure that the leashes don't get tangled up. A tangled leash can cause fear and unwanted aggression. If things get aggressive, then you can quickly yank your dog away from the other animal without damaging its neck.

Play style

Understanding your dog's play style is important when introducing them to other animals. Maltese typically fall within the Toy Group play style. This play style encompasses small dog breeds like Pomeranians, Pugs, and Shih-Tzus. Dogs within this play style generally crave attention and don't like to be left by themselves. It's common for them to enjoy sitting in the arms of their owners more than running around with other dogs.

The Toy Group play style tends to be cat-like. They use their paws to bat at your face or arms to signal to you that they want more belly scratches. The Toy Group is also known for playing fetch but not bringing the ball back. Dogs like Maltese tend to play best with other dogs in the Toy Group.

Micah fits perfectly within the Toy Group play style. He loves sitting on our laps and rarely plays with other dogs, even at the dog park. He prefers human interaction over interaction with other animals. In fact, he leaves

Photo Courtesy of Judith Hough

other dogs alone completely. Even when we try to take Micah to the dog park, he is constantly trying to jump up into our arms.

The herding group

This group is comprised of breeds like Border Collies and Australian Shepherds. These dogs were specifically bred over the years to herd livestock. They tend to stare, stalk, and nip at the heels of other dogs when playing. They are highly energetic and require a large amount of mental stimulation to keep them happy. This means that they instinctively chase and run after other animals. This may be intimidating to your Maltese.

The sporting group

This group is comprised of breeds like Black Labs and German Short-Haired Pointers. They were bred specifically to locate and hunt down game. Breeds like Cocker Spaniels were bred to scare prey out of bushes for a clear shot. Dogs within this group are rowdy and love the water. They like playing "find it" games where they have to use their scavenger skill set. Beware of dog breeds in the sporting group that may think your tiny little Maltese is game similar to a rabbit.

The terrier group

This group is comprised of breeds like Bull Terriers, American Pit Bull Terriers, and Jack Russell Terriers. They were bred to hunt underground prey such as prairie dogs and other crop-invading pests. They are feisty and energetic and love to dig. They tend to be overly enthusiastic about ripping up chew toys. They enjoy wrestling and using their stumpy bodies to push other animals around. Maltese and other members of the Toy Group get along well with the Terrier Group as long as they are not overly aggressive.

The hound group

This group is comprised of breeds like Beagles, Basset Hounds, and Dachshunds. They can be found with their nose to the ground, following the trail of a scent. They were selectively bred as tracking animals and are pack-oriented. They generally get along with all other breeds and keep to themselves. They're more interested in sniffing around than roughhousing.

The working group

This group is comprised of breeds like Siberian Huskies and Golden Retrievers. They were selectively bred to perform a task. It consists of German Shepherd police dogs, Golden Retriever service animals, bomb-sniffing dogs, or sled-pulling Siberian Huskies. These dogs are usually very smart and require a high amount of mental stimulation to keep them happy. Due to the variation in activity bred for, these dogs can be unpredictable, and you should keep a close eye on them at the dog park. They are generally well-behaved and obedient.

The dog park

Now that you understand different play styles, it's safe to take your Maltese to the dog park. Do not take your Maltese to the dog park if it is not current with its vaccines. Without the proper vaccinations, you are putting both your dog and others at risk.

Start by researching dog parks in your area. Read reviews of each dog park to see if the park is a good fit for you. Red flags to look out for include complaints of violent dogs, filthiness, and a poorly landscaped play area. Keep in mind that some dog parks close seasonally and will also be closed after storm events to prevent damage to their grounds. Drive to your prospective dog park and inspect it before you take your Maltese to see if it's a good fit.

Although most dog parks are off-leash, some dog parks are on-leash. If your Maltese hasn't had much social interaction yet, then it is best to take it to an on-leash park to start. You'll have more control over your dog at an on-leash park in case things don't go as planned.

Some dog parks have separate areas reserved for different-sized dogs. Read the signs carefully at each dog park and make sure that you take your Maltese into the "small dog" area. Dog parks strategically separate small dogs from large dogs to prevent injury. If your dog park has both large breeds and small breeds mixed together, then you'll have to remain extra vigilant to make sure your Maltese doesn't get injured by a larger dog.

Once you arrive at your dog park, it's best to keep your Maltese on a leash at first. Carefully observe the interactions between the other dogs and stay away from dogs that are playing too rough. Introduce your Maltese on-leash to other dogs at the park to feel it out. If everyone seems to be getting along alright, then it is safe to let your dog off-leash.

By the time you take your Maltese to the dog park, you should have practiced basic commands so that your Maltese doesn't turn into the troublemaker. Commands that are important to know at the dog park include "come," "stay," "down," and "leave it." Remember to be courteous to other dogs and their owners and always keep your Maltese under control.

Other courtesies include cleaning up after your dog. Most dog parks have plastic bags and garbage bins to dispose of feces, but you should bring extra plastic poop bags just in case there aren't any left in the dispenser. You should also bring a water dish to keep your Maltese healthy and hydrated.

Maltese and cats

Maltese tend to get along well with cats. That said, how well a Maltese and a cat get along is entirely dependent upon each of the animal's individual personalities.

Researchers have identified five main cat personalities that are important to recognize as a Maltese owner: neuroticism, dominance, impulsiveness, agreeableness, and extraversion. Cats with neurotic and dominant personalities may not get along well with your Maltese. Impulsive cats may be best friends with your Maltese one second and at its throat the next. Agreeable and extraverted cats will get along just fine with your pup.

House cats can be territorial with their space. It's best to introduce your Maltese and cat in a neutral area such as a friend's house or a park. This way, you aren't forcing the animals to interact in an environment where the cat feels inclined to protect its space. Before you bring your Maltese home, it's advisable to set up a room or space that each animal can feel comfortable in and separate from one another just in case you need to separate them.

Veterinarians and professional pet trainers suggest scent swapping. This way, you can introduce the two pets without physically meeting. To scent swap, just rub a piece of clothing all over the cat and a separate piece of clothing all over the Maltese. Introduce each animal to each other through their respective scents on the clothing. Cats and dogs alike use scents to recall and identify their environment, people, and even other animals. With the help of scent swapping, your pets will be familiar with each other before even meeting.

When you first bring the Maltese or cat home, allow the newcomer some time to familiarize itself with your home before the introduction. You want your new pet as comfortable as possible in its new space so that it can relax and unwind. The more comfortable your new pet is in its home, the less likely it is to be on edge when introduced to its new companion. Another tip is to make sure that your pets are both well-exercised before the introduction. This way, they won't have any pent-up energy or aggression and will be too tired to do anything erratic.

Now it's time for the introduction itself! Start by placing both pets in the same room but don't force them to interact. If you followed through with scent swapping, then the two animals should immediately recognize one

Photo Courtesy of Austin Parsons

another. Be sure to pet both animals and allow them to smell each other's scent on your hands. By smelling each other's scent on your hands, they begin to develop trust.

It's crucial to keep calm during this initial meeting. Animals can sense fear and tension. Use a calm and soothing voice to communicate but be stern where necessary. It's important to make your expectations clear to your pets up-front. You will not tolerate aggression but invite calmness. It's best to keep the two animals separate. Don't force them together into an uncomfortable situation. The first step is to get them to be comfortable enough to be in the same room with one another. The second step is to get them comfortable with physical interaction.

Be sure to reward both animals for good behavior. Give your pets treats for not growling or hissing. If things are going well, then you can allow the two pets to approach one another. The first physical interaction is the most important, so pay close attention. If your cat starts hissing or your Maltese starts angrily growling, then it's best to separate them from one another until they get more comfortable.

Keep the first physical introduction as short as possible. Don't allow one pet to start bullying the other with its body weight or other methods of intimidation. Most importantly, start slowly and don't force anything. Let their interactions occur organically for the best chance at success.

Micah has only met one other cat in his life. The cat had a neurotic personality and simply stood in the corner and stared at him. Micah was highly intimidated by the cat, who was the same size as him, if not bigger. Micah's Toy Group play style showed its colors almost immediately. Micah wanted to be as close to his owners as possible and even jumped up into my lap.

Maltese and small animals

Micah may not have any cat siblings at home, but he gets along amazingly well with our guinea pig. Our guinea pig's cage is made of wire and sits on the floor. Micah could easily jump over the cage and attack the guinea pig if he wanted to but has no desire. Instead, Micah gently sniffs at the guinea pig through the cage and playfully chases it around the house when it's time to clean its cage.

Thanks to the Maltese's Toy Group play style and low prey drive, they are rarely aggressive towards small animals. You should still exert caution with small rodents like mice, pet rats, and hamsters, though. Dogs have instinctively hunted these creatures in the wild over the years, so it's best not to leave your Maltese unattended near small rodents just to be safe.

Small animals should be introduced to your Maltese while you hold them. Your Maltese will likely barrage the small animal with a sniffing attack, but nothing more. If your Maltese is trained and listens to commands such as "no bite," then you have very little to worry about. In fact, you should be more worried about the small animal biting back out of fear. Despite their small size, small animals can deliver a powerful bite that can break the skin and lead to an infection.

Maltese and humans

Socializing your Maltese with humans shouldn't be much of a problem thanks to the breed's docile and peaceful nature. Despite their docile and peaceful nature, it's important to prepare your Maltese for socializing scenarios such as with kids and men.

Photo Courtesy of Lori Hoel

Maltese and men

Some Maltese are instinctively fearful of men. If your Maltese was adopted, then this could be a result of an abusive previous owner. For a majority of dogs, a fear of men stems from a lack of socialization as a puppy. From a dog's perspective, men tend to be larger, have deeper voices, and intimidating features such as beards.

If your dog has an instinctive fear of men, then you need to address it as soon as possible before it progresses. Invite a man over such as a friend, family member, or significant other, and begin training immediately. Don't push the dog out of its comfort zone and let all the interactions happen organically. Let your dog approach the man, not vice versa, and use words of encouragement to cheer your Maltese on. Let the man offer treats to encourage the interaction and gain trust without forcing it.

While your Maltese may never feel completely comfortable around men, it's crucial to train them to a point where they don't show signs of aggression when in the same room as men. If your Maltese continues to be aggressive towards men, then you may need to hire a trainer and keep your Maltese completely separated from men in the meantime.

Maltese and kids

Babies, toddlers, and young children should never be left unattended with your Maltese. Parents should work towards educating their children about how to behave around dogs to prevent an unpleasant encounter. Unfortunately, if a bite does occur, the fault always falls back on the dog and its owner.

Parents should teach their children that dogs may not like tight hugs and kisses. Children need to understand that pulling the dog's hair is not allowed. Other tips include not approaching the dog when it is eating, not taking anything away from the dog like a toy or bone, and leaving dogs alone that are sleeping or relaxing.

Your Maltese should be well-trained before interacting with any small children. It should know key commands such as "sit," "stay," "down," and "leave it." Another important command is "no lick." Small children may be intimidated by your Maltese's kisses and think that it is trying to bite them.

CHAPTER 11
Dealing With Unwanted Behavior

"Keep in mind that many 'cute' behaviors from a puppy may seem adorable now, but will not seem the same coming from an adult. Therefore, don't allow your puppy to do anything you wouldn't want your adult dog to do."

KAREN ORSIN
Petite Pups

Let's face it: at some point in your Maltese's life, you're going to have to deal with unwanted behavior. Whether it's chewing, barking, whining, stubbornness, or aggression, dogs are instinctual creatures that need training to fit within our domesticated lifestyles. It's important to deal with unwanted behavior with positive reinforcement rather than punishment. By rewarding your dog for good behavior rather than punishing it for bad behavior, you develop a close bond and trust. Exercising patience and consistency when dealing with unwanted behavior is the best way to get rid of it.

Chewing

Chewing is one of the most common unwanted behaviors that drive pet owners crazy. Chewing on unwanted items is most commonly observed in puppies but can carry on into adulthood if left untrained. Adopted Maltese who came from a bad home may also have chewing issues. It's much more difficult to train an adult Maltese to stop chewing than a puppy Maltese.

Puppies go through teething phases where chewing on things helps soothe the pain of new teeth poking through their gums. Adult dogs are also inclined to chew on things as it's nature's way of cleaning their teeth and strengthening their jaws. Lastly, chewing is mentally stimulating and combats boredom.

Photo Courtesy of Joan Ryan

With all of the above in mind, here are some tips to get your Maltese to stop chewing on unwanted items:

- **PAY ATTENTION:** Much like you would with a toddler, pay close attention to your Maltese throughout the day. Dogs are curious by nature. Since they don't have hands and thumbs, they interact with the physical world with their mouth. By closely observing your Maltese throughout the day, you can stop the bad behavior as soon as it begins or even before it happens. Try throwing a toy around when your Maltese gets noticeably anxious to distract it from chewing on unwanted items.
- **PUPPY PROOF YOUR HOME:** Remove small and chewable items from areas where your Maltese can reach them. That means putting your shoes away in a closet and moving the remote control onto a high tabletop. This is more difficult if your dog is chewing on things like cords. Try hiding and blocking access to electrical cords, if possible. If that's not possible, then consider purchasing NaturVet's Bitter Yuck! It's a bitter and nontoxic spray that you can put on your cords to prevent your Maltese from chewing on them.
- **DOG TOYS:** If your Maltese destroys plush toys by ripping out the stuffing, then consider buying tougher toys or replace them with bones. The plush within stuffed toys can be a choking hazard for puppies or even an adult Maltese. There are many dog toys on the market that are designed to be both chewable and indestructible. If you catch your Maltese chewing on an unwanted item, then try replacing it with a chewable item. You must train your Maltese to chew on toys rather than shoes.
- **DAILY EXERCISE:** Maltese that are bored are more likely to chew on unwanted objects. Take your dog on daily walks and play with it for at least 15 minutes per day. It's in both of your best interests to tire out your dog. Maltese need mental stimulation and may display bad behavior out of boredom or excess energy.

Micah never had any issues with chewing on unwanted items, but he did have issues with chewing on hands and feet. It was the only way that he knew how to play. He would unintentionally bite too hard and never knew when to stop. To train him out of this behavior, any time that he would try chewing on our hands, we would replace our hands with a chew toy. After a while, Micah went straight to the chew toy instead of our hands.

Photo Courtesy of Lu Crabtree

Barking

It's important to draw a fine line between regular barking and excessive barking. Much like our own voices as humans, dogs vocalize to express themselves. Though Maltese don't have barking issues like some other dog breeds, it's cruel to expect your Maltese to be always silent.

Here are some tips to get your Maltese to stop barking excessively:

- **GET RID OF THE MOTIVATION:** It's unlikely that your Maltese is barking at nothing. Try to figure out what your Maltese is barking at, and then remove the motivation. Let's say that your Maltese barks at cars that drive by your house during the day. Simply shut the blinds or put your dog in a different room so that it can no longer see the cars. If your Maltese barks at other dogs during walks, then distract them while the other dog passes by or head in a different direction.
- **IGNORE IT:** This may be easier said than done, but sometimes it is best to just ignore the barking. As long as the barking isn't disrupting a neighbor or anyone within your house, then it's okay to allow your dog to use its voice. Immediately reward your dog with a treat or praise once it stops barking. After a while, your Maltese may catch on that being quiet is rewarded with attention or treats.
- **INCOMPATIBLE BEHAVIORS:** Professional dog trainers recommend commanding your dog to do a trick while it is having a barking episode. This works best when someone is knocking at your front door, for example. Simply command your dog to sit or lie down. Your dog will have trouble multitasking and barking while obeying your command.
- **DAILY EXERCISE:** Much like with chewing, dogs bark out of boredom and pent-up energy. Try taking your Maltese for daily walks and play with it for at least 15 minutes per day. Maltese are less likely to expend energy barking if they are tired from a long walk.

Micah barks incessantly at pedestrians as they walk by my house. I choose to ignore it for the most part since it isn't bothering anyone. Micah used to bark at other dogs on his walks, and that is where I drew the line. As we walk by other dogs on a leash, I stop Micah and have him sit. While sitting, I try to distract Micah and remind him that he is a good boy for not barking. It took a long time to train this unwanted behavior out of Micah, but consistency and patience prevailed.

Whining/crying

Whining is one of the most annoying unwanted behaviors as it is usually synonymous with begging. Whining at the door to go potty outside is good behavior that should be praised. Crying for food is unwanted behavior and should not be allowed.

You should never feed your Maltese human food from the table. This develops bad habits and creates unrealistic expectations for your dog. Your Maltese will start to believe that he or she is entitled to human food whenever you eat. If you don't feed your Maltese off the plate, then they will start whining and begging. Dogs have an enhanced sense of smell, so that slice of pizza that you think smells delicious is even more enticing for your Maltese. Once your Maltese has a taste for human food, it will want more and more

Photo Courtesy of Stacy Payne

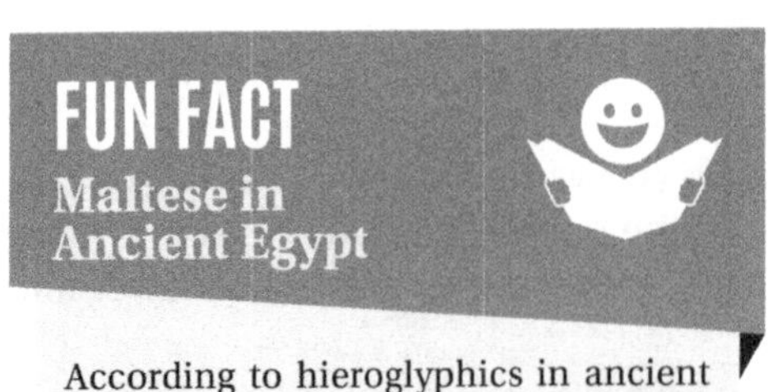

According to hieroglyphics in ancient Egypt, the ancient Egyptians believed that Maltese dogs had the power of healing. Supposedly, these dogs would sometimes be placed in bedrooms because it was believed that they could heal people while they were sleeping.

and will continue to cry until it gets it. It's best to sternly tell your Maltese "no" once it starts begging for food and then ignore his whimpers entirely.

Your Maltese may also whine because it's seeking attention. Maltese are generally low-energy dogs and don't need as much mental stimulation as other dogs. If your Maltese is whining out of the blue, then take it for a walk or play with it.

Understanding why your Maltese is whining is important. Whining for food or excessively whining for attention is clearly bad behavior, but there are other reasons as to why your dog could be whining. If you notice that your Maltese is crying but cannot figure out why, then it could possibly be in pain, anxious, or afraid. Pain, anxiety, or fear is usually coupled with yawning, licking, or averting the eyes.

Micah only whines when he has to go potty outside. He has become privy to the fact that he is rewarded with a treat whenever he goes outside. Sometimes, Micah whines by the door and once we let him outside, we find out that he didn't have to go to the bathroom after all. He was simply trying to trick us into giving him a treat.

Prey drive

When compared to other dog breeds, Maltese have one of the lowest prey drives. A low prey drive is what makes Maltese such great apartment pets. It contributes to their docile nature. Dog trainers use the term prey drive when talking about dogs that are alert and easily trained. Dogs with higher prey drives tend to pay more attention and are easier to train. Dogs with low prey drives simply don't have the motivation.

That said, some Maltese may still have issues with prey drive. The only way to mitigate prey drive in a dog is through distraction. You'll have to do behavioral work to establish control and divert attention, encouraging eye contact, training your Maltese to stay, and removing your dog from the prey.

Stubborn moments

The low prey drive of the Maltese can lead to stubbornness. It can be frustrating at first, but we must understand that a Maltese's behavior doesn't conform to our own standards of good manners. When training your Maltese, it can sometimes feel like you are losing the battle of wills. An example is when you command your Maltese to come, but it chooses to lie down instead.

If a dog isn't overtly responsive to your commands at first, it's important to remain patient and consistent. Try training your stubborn Maltese in an area free of distractions like a living room. Put toys or other distractions away so that your Maltese doesn't become sidetracked. It's possible that your Maltese is coming off as stubborn, but it is just nervous. Maltese are gentle, docile, and occasionally nervous. Avoid punishing your dog for stubbornness as it may just increase its anxiety.

Even the most stubborn dog will cave in for the right reward. Try rewarding your stubborn Maltese with treats, belly rubs, or even walks. Different dogs value different things, so you will have to figure out what motivates your Maltese, whether it's a favorite toy or some peanut butter. If you've tried everything and your dog is still stubborn, then it's best to hire a professional trainer to help you.

Micah is entirely motivated by food. He can be stubborn at times, but if you dangle a treat in front of him, he will do just about anything.

Dog aggression

To address aggression issues in a Maltese, you must first understand the root of the aggression. Adopted dogs may be dealing with post-traumatic stress caused by a previous owner. Perhaps the dog was abused. Its aggression could be stemming from distrust. In this case, you'll have to slowly build up trust with the dog. There are five different types of aggression in dogs to understand:

1. **TERRITORIAL:** For Maltese displaying territorial aggression, you will need to establish control by having your dog sit and stay until it calms down. Most Maltese are instinctually territorial and protect the front door and the yard. If you're having issues with your Maltese exhibiting territorial aggression to guests at your front door, then you may have to remove your dog from the area to provide safety for your visitors.

Photo Courtesy of Marie-Michelle Chiasson

② **PROTECTIVE:** Some Maltese become so closely bonded to their owners or siblings that they may become protective. To deal with this behavior, you have to establish trust with what your Maltese is protecting. If the Maltese is protecting another dog, then stay calm and use a soothing voice to gain your dog's trust. Don't make any sudden movements that could scare the Maltese into aggressive behavior.

3. **POSSESSIVE:** Possessive aggression stems from protecting a favorite toy or bone. It could also come from protecting a food dish. Possessive aggression in Maltese could stem from living life on the street as a stray if your Maltese was adopted. As a stray, your Maltese may have had to protect its belongings with its life. It will take patience and trust-building to rid your Maltese of possessive behaviors.
4. **FEAR:** If you back any animal into a corner, it will likely bite. All living creatures have a fight or flight response system built into their DNA. If a dog is backed into a corner, being bullied by another dog, or being beaten, then it may not see any other way of escaping the situation aside from violence. Adopted Maltese with a history of abuse may be aggressive out of fear. You'll need to be patient and build trust with the dog until it settles into your home and opens up to you.
5. **SOCIAL:** Social aggression is instinctual. Many species of animals roughhouse in the wild to play. Roughhousing isn't only just fun, but it also helps prepare wild animals for real altercations. Playing rough with other dogs is okay, but you should be prepared to step in if your Maltese is being overly aggressive.

Aggressive behavior is nothing to be taken lightly. Once you understand the root of your Maltese's aggression, you can begin to address it. If your Maltese bites a pedestrian or another dog, it could be put down for bad behavior. Take any signs of aggression seriously and begin training immediately.

As with the rest of the unwanted behaviors, training away aggression takes patience and consistency. Most aggression stems from trust issues, so it is important to rebuild trust through positive reinforcement and to eliminate punishment altogether. If you're still having trouble with aggression, then you should call your veterinarian or seek out a professional dog trainer.

CHAPTER 12
Nutrition

"Maltese dogs are prone to hypoglycemia and need to pick and graze throughout the day. They can be very picky eaters and require a nutrient dense diet. Choosing the right food that produces a firm stool is essential to anal gland health. They're very sensitive to too much fat so table scraps and people food should be avoided. Maltese dogs also have 'stress tummy', meaning that if they're stressed, they'll show you by vomiting and/or diarrhea. Choose a food specially formulated for toy dogs and 'free feed', meaning always have food available."

BARBARA SHEWMAKE
Storybook Maltese

The dog food market is oversaturated, and it can be difficult to decide which food is best for your Maltese among the competition. The diet of your Maltese has a direct impact on its short- and long-term health. It's important to feed your Maltese food that has a healthy balance of the right nutrients.

> **HELPFUL TIP**
> **Supplements For a Healthy Coat**
>
> 
>
> If you own a Maltese, the chances are that you want to keep your dog's coat looking as healthy and luxurious as possible. Omega-3 fatty acids are vital to your dog's healthy diet and are essential for heart, fur, and joint health. This healthy fat is not naturally produced by dogs and therefore needs to be obtained through diet. Many dog foods are enriched with Omega-3, and supplements can also be given. Be sure to speak with your vet before introducing any supplements into your dog's diet.

Maltese from 2 to 4 pounds should eat from one-quarter cup to half a cup of food per day. Maltese over 5 pounds should eat half a cup to three-quarters of a cup per day. Consult with your veterinarian for dietary recommendations. There isn't a one size fits all approach when it comes to feeding your Maltese, as your pup's diet will depend upon health, allergies, size, and activity level.

Dry or wet food?

Both dry food and wet food are capable of providing your Maltese with the nutrition that they need to live a long and happy life. Dry foods, otherwise referred to as kibble, cost less than wet food. Wet food, otherwise referred to as canned food, is more expensive but more flavorful. If it were up to your Maltese, it would probably choose to eat wet food over dry food.

Depending on the brand, wet dog food can contain real chunks of proteins like chicken, as well as sliced vegetables like carrots. Wet dog food tends to contain more meat protein than kibble and has fewer carbohydrates. The air-tight packaging of canned dog food is free from potentially harmful synthetic preservatives. Wet dog food also has a higher moisture content, which can help dieting dogs feel fuller faster.

That same high moisture content can lead to runny bowels. Because of this, dogs with stomach or bowel issues may be better off sticking to kibble. If you choose to free-feed your Maltese, meaning you leave food out in a bowl all day and allow your dog to eat at will, then dry dog food is the way to go. It doesn't have to be refrigerated once opened and won't spoil like wet food.

I feed Micah a combination of wet and dry food. He gets one small portion of wet food in the morning, and then we allow him to free-feed from kibble throughout the day. Micah loves wet dog food and eats it all up immediately. We rotate between brands of wet dog food so that he gets a variety of nutrients and flavors.

You can't go wrong with either wet dog food or dry dog food as long as it is well-balanced. Whichever you choose, you should avoid brands that use fillers, artificial additives, generic meat sources, and animal by-products. You should look for foods with real meat sources that support joint health and cognitive function.

Photo Courtesy of Irina Korovyakovskaya

Grain or grain-free food?

For many years, grain-free food was the go-to recommendation from veterinarians. Food with grain is thought to trigger intolerances or allergies within dogs. Recently, though, grain-free diets have been linked to a heart disease in dogs called dilated cardiomyopathy (DCM). There isn't quite enough research out there to prove that grain-free diets cause heart problems, but it's recommended that you stick with a grain diet unless your dog has an intolerance or allergies, just in case.

Raw diet

Raw dog food diets are highly controversial, but their popularity continues to rise. The raw diet focuses on raw meat, bones, fruits, and vegetables. Racing dogs and other working dogs like sled dogs have thrived on raw diets but may be harmful to smaller domesticated dogs like Maltese.

The potential benefits of a raw food diet include a shinier coat, healthier skin, healthier teeth, and higher energy levels. Showroom Maltese would greatly benefit from a raw diet. Risks include bacterial infections, stomach issues, and intestinal issues. There is also a potential for your Maltese to choke on bones, break teeth, or puncture an internal organ.

A raw diet consists mainly of meat still on the bone, whole or ground bones, organ meats like livers, raw eggs, raw vegetables like broccoli and spinach, fruits like apples, and dairy such as yogurts. A raw diet is also considerably more expensive and requires close attention to detail to make sure that your Maltese is eating a balanced diet.

Puppy dog food

As soon as your Maltese puppy is weaned off of mother's milk, it's crucial to start a feeding plan that lays a foundation for a healthy adulthood. A balanced diet as a puppy helps the dog grow at a healthy rate, primes its immune system, and prevents orthopedic issues.

There are four main nutrients to keep in mind when feeding your puppy: proteins, fats, calcium, and carbohydrates. A healthy balance of each nutrient will encourage optimal growth and prevent obesity. Each nutrient is broken down below:

Photo Courtesy of Joan Ryan

- **PROTEIN:** Puppies need a much higher amount of protein than adults. This need steadily decreases until adulthood. A healthy protein range is anywhere from 22-32%. This range should not be exceeded.
- **FAT:** Fatty acids are essential to a healthy pup. Fat carries fat-soluble vitamins that help with energy levels and mass. A healthy range is anywhere between 10-25% and should not be exceeded. Risks of exceeding include obesity and orthopedic issues.
- **CALCIUM:** Small breeds like Maltese aren't as sensitive to over or under-feeding calcium as large breeds, but it should still be monitored. A healthy intake of calcium will lead to healthy joints and bones. A healthy range of calcium ranges from 0.7% to 1.7%.
- **CARBOHYDRATES:** Carbohydrates must be digestible. The appropriate range of carbohydrates to maximize your puppy's health is 20%.

Adult dog food

When your Maltese reaches 90% of its expected adult weight, then it is considered an adult and should be switched to adult food. This is typically around the seven-month mark. Adult dogs require less protein, less fat, and less calcium. Their nutritional needs are broken down below:

- **PROTEIN:** Adult Maltese need approximately 18% protein in their diets.
- **FAT:** Adult Maltese need significantly less fat than puppies. They only need around 5%, or they are at risk for obesity.
- **CALCIUM:** The healthy range of calcium for an adult Maltese is .5%.
- **CARBOHYDRATES:** Carbohydrate intake varies depending on your Maltese's activity level and current health. Obese Maltese should consume less, while emaciated Maltese should consume more. A healthy range is 30%.

Treats

Dog treats play a crucial role in the development of your Maltese. They are used to reward your pup during housebreaking, while learning tricks, and for overall great behavior. Dog treats can also be used as a nutritional supplement to deliver vitamins and minerals that your dog may not be getting from its food otherwise. Much like with wet and dry dog food, there are certain ingredients that should be avoided if possible:

- Artificial colors and flavors

- Preservatives
- Cereal grains
- High levels of corn or soy
- Animal by-products
- Generic meat sources
- Rawhides or pig's ears that are hard to digest

Treats should be given in moderation in accordance with your Maltese's balanced diet. Look for treats with all-natural ingredients and real meat, vegetables, cheese, and fruits.

We give Micah small, bite-sized treats so that they don't conflict with his diet. Micah also always has a rawhide-free bone to chew on throughout the day. We occasionally give him special dental bone treats to help freshen up his breath and clean his teeth.

Photo Courtesy of Karen Crawford

Supplements

Photo Courtesy of Peggy Summitt

The best way for your Maltese to get its nutrients is through a healthy and balanced diet. However, there may be some instances where your dog needs additional nutrients through the form of supplements. Supplements can treat a range of issues, including arthritis, joint stiffness, heart health, digestion, and coat care. Below is a list of the most commonly used supplements:

- **GLUCOSAMINE:** An amino sugar that helps build cartilage, glucosamine helps relieve joint pain and improve mobility in senior dogs.
- **FISH OIL:** This supplement contains omega-3 fatty acids that improve the quality of your Maltese's coat and alleviates skin allergies. Fish oil helps give show dogs' fur an extra shine. Fish oil is also useful for arthritis, heart health, joint health, and brain health. Micah occasionally develops a limp after a long hike, and an omega-3 supplement has him feeling as good as new in no time at all.
- **ANTIOXIDANTS:** Antioxidants are believed to counteract the effect of aging as it relates to cognitive function and memory loss. They reduce inflammation by protecting the body from free radicals that can damage cell membranes and lead to cellular death.
- **PROBIOTICS:** Probiotics support intestinal, digestive, and stomach health. It's used to treat diarrhea, vomiting, and gas. Probiotics live naturally in the form of yeast and live bacteria cultures.

CHAPTER 13
Health

Breeding purebreds like Maltese does not come without its consequences. Due to a lack of genetic diversity and inbreeding, purebred Maltese have heightened health issues such as tear staining, heart problems, congenital liver issues, encephalitis, dental issues, and patellar luxation. Parasites such as ticks, fleas, and worms may also infect your Maltese at some point in its life.

Photo Courtesy of Marie-Michelle Chiasson

Tear staining

"A grain-free diet and no dye in the dog food can help reduce tear stains."

LEONA LUPULESKU
Leona's Maltese

Tear staining is a common problem in Maltese. It's a reddish-brown discoloration underneath the eyes that shows up distinctly on a Maltese's white hair. It's caused by excessive moisture coming from the eyes. This excessive tear production is called epiphora. The reddish-brown discoloration is actually yeast growing within the moisture.

It's important to see a veterinarian if your Maltese has tear-staining issues. There could be an underlying medical issue such as ingrown eyelashes, an eye infection, large tear glands, blocked tear ducts, glaucoma, or an inverted eyelid. Ear infections and dental issues can also trigger excessive tearing in Maltese.

If an underlying medical issue is ruled out, then it is likely a genetic issue. You should do your best to keep your Maltese's eyes moisture-free. Make it a routine to clean and dry off your Maltese's eyes on a nightly basis. There are over-the-counter medications that can help with tear staining. Be sure to avoid anything that bleaches the fur or contains antibiotics.

Heart problems

Heart problems such as heart murmurs or congestive heart failure are unfortunately common amongst Maltese and other purebred dogs. It's most commonly observed in senior dogs ten and older. Heart murmurs don't display any observable physical side effects, so it usually goes by unnoticed. Your veterinarian should be checking your Maltese's heart during its annual checkups.

Heart murmurs may lead to congestive heart failure if left untreated. Murmurs are graded from 1 through 6, with 6 being the most severe. No treatment is necessary for murmurs from grades 1 through 3. As murmurs progress, your Maltese could develop issues with breathing, coughing, and exercise tolerance. Try switching your Maltese to a low-sodium diet to help lower blood pressure.

Congenital liver issues

"Maltese can get a condition called liver shunt. It can be hereditary so know your breeders lines. It can also just occur with no known cause. Most cases can be cured with surgery and usually shows up in the first year of life so be sure your breeder gives a health guarantee covering at least 1 year."

KAREN ORSIN
Petite Pups

Liver shunts, also referred to as portosystemic shunts, are a congenital liver issue that impacts the flow of blood to the liver. The liver filters toxins from the blood, and when blood does not properly enter the liver, toxins can bypass the liver and poison the body. Mild liver shunts may go by unnoticed, but more severe shunts cause symptoms such as stunted growth, diarrhea, constipation, drooling, seizures, and may even be fatal.

Surgery is the only effective treatment for liver shunts. The liver shunt must be surgically closed to prevent blood from bypassing the liver. Surgery has a high success rate with just one shunt but is at an increased risk of failure if multiple shunts present themselves.

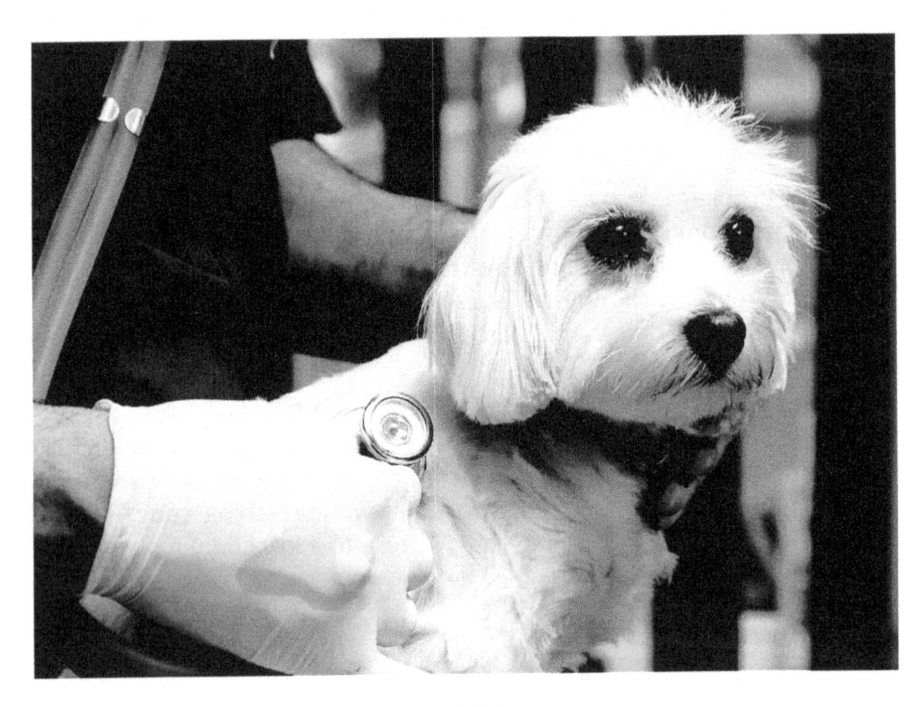

Encephalitis

Also referred to as GME, encephalitis is an inflammatory autoimmune disease that attacks the central nervous system. It comes on quickly and is life-threatening if not addressed. Symptoms of GME include blindness, drowsiness, circling, seizures, behavioral changes, weakness, head pressing, neck pain, and imbalance. GME is diagnosed by bloodwork, which should also be used to rule out organ issues.

QUOTE

"Apparently, all I do is walk my dogs. In L.A. I have more of a yard existence, and so I enjoy walking my two little dogs in New York—one's a Maltese and one's a Shih Tzu."

Jim Parsons,
American actor

If left untreated, GME can lead to death. Treatment is aggressive and includes high doses of steroids. Once stabilized, the dog is treated with a combination of immunosuppressive steroids and even chemotherapy drugs.

Dental care

"Periodontal disease and gingivitis can cause a serious bacterial infection that can spread through the bloodstream to the kidneys, liver, heart or brain. Periodontal disease is irreversible, so now is a great time to get started on a regular oral-care regimen with your puppy. Prevention is the key to keeping your puppy healthy, happy and living a long life."

LEONA LUPULESKU
Leona's Maltese

Keeping your Maltese's mouth clean is important for your dog's teeth, gums, and even breath. Adult Maltese have 42 tiny teeth that need to be cleaned of plaque, which eventually hardens into tartar. Tartar has a yellow or brown tint and is difficult to remove without the proper tools. Tartar and plaque slowly destroy the tooth enamel and weaken it.

Tooth decay can lead to tooth rot and infection. Decayed teeth may rot and fall out if left uncared for. Periodontal disease and gingivitis are most commonly observed in Maltese with dental issues. Tooth decay, periodontal disease, and gingivitis can all be painful and unpleasant for your Maltese.

Chew toys such as dental bones help naturally brush your Maltese's teeth free of plaque. Dental bones will also help fight off gingivitis and unwanted bad breath. Some veterinarians recommend feeding your dog dry kibble as the abrasion helps clean your dog's teeth. You can also brush your Maltese's teeth with a canine-sized toothbrush and a dental spray.

Veterinarians offer full teeth cleanings and comprehensive dental exams. Unfortunately, your pup must be sedated. Because of this, unless your dog is suffering from tooth decay or any other dental issue, you should avoid having your dog sedated and stick to at-home care.

Photo Courtesy of Michelle Lewis

Luxated patellas

Luxated patellas are one of the most commonly observed physical health issues in Maltese. It's a condition where the kneecap slips out of the groove and dislocates. It's an inherited congenital disorder that becomes worse over time. Luxated patellas can develop as early as within the first year of your Maltese's life. It may occur in multiple knees and is commonly mistaken for a regular injury.

There are a few different reasons that this happens: Ligaments that are supposed to hold the patellas in place may be underdeveloped and weakened, the patella itself could be too shallow, or the tibia could be improperly aligned. Most cases are mild and don't require surgery, but extreme cases could lead to pain and lameness.

Ticks

Ticks live in dark and damp areas. They can be found anywhere from the woods nearby on your walks, in the grass in your backyard, or even the dog park. Heavily wooded areas and tall grasses are where your Maltese is most at risk for ticks.

The best way to prevent ticks is to avoid heavily wooded areas and tall grasses during peak tick seasons. Ticks are most abundant in the springtime during their mating season. There are also over-the-counter medications and ointments that you can apply to your dog that deter ticks. Oral medications, topical medications, and even tick collars are all safe and effective for preventing ticks.

You should make it a habit to inspect for ticks after taking your dog outside. Ticks gravitate towards warm and dark areas on your Maltese as well. Common places that ticks like to hide include under the front legs, inside the groin, between the toes, under the ears, around the eyelids, and under the collar.

Preventing a tick bite will prevent tick-borne diseases such as Lyme disease, Rocky Mountain Spotted Fever, and Ehrlichiosis. If your Maltese was bit by a tick and displays signs of a rash, fever, lameness, loss of appetite, lethargy, bruising, or vomiting, then take it to see a veterinarian as soon as possible. Ticks can transmit their diseases in as little as 36 hours, so it's important to get them removed immediately.

It's best to take your Maltese to a veterinarian to have the tick professionally removed. To remove a tick at home, first, wear gloves to avoid contact with blood if the tick is already engorged. Grab the tick with sharp tweezers as close to the skin as possible. Quickly and carefully tug the tick up and away from the skin to remove it. Check to see that the head of the tick did not break off and is not still attached to your Maltese. Dispose of the tick down the toilet and monitor your pup for signs of illness for the next several days.

Fleas

Fleas can be transmitted from dogs at the dog park or even picked up in nature if they are left behind by deer or other animals. If your Maltese is noticeably itching, then inspect it for fleas. Adult fleas can grow up to one inch in size and are easily visible to the naked eye. Fleas leave behind "flea dirt," which looks like little specks of pepper on your Maltese's skin.

Other signs include hair loss, irritated skin, or pale gums. Flea eggs may also be observed on furniture, and they eventually hatch into flea larvae. Flea eggs are very small, white, and ovular in shape.

If your Maltese is infected with fleas, then give it a bath using lukewarm water and a special flea shampoo as recommended by your veterinarian. You should then comb your dog's hair with a fine-tooth flea comb. Dunk the fleas that stick to the flea comb in hot water to kill them. Continue to inspect your Maltese for fleas at least once per week until no more fleas are observed.

Photo Courtesy of Irina Korovyakovskaya

Worms

There are five main species of worms that commonly infect Maltese: roundworms, tapeworms, hookworms, whipworms, and heartworms. If left untreated, parasitic worms can lead to organ failure and even death. It's important to take your dog's stool sample to the vet once per year to check for worms.

Worms are mainly transmitted through the feces of other animals. If your dog sniffs another dog's pile of poop on a walk, then that is one way that it could have gotten worms. Worms like heartworms are

Photo Courtesy of Kathleen Engelen

transmitted via mosquitoes as larva. Once matured, the heartworms wreak havoc in your Maltese's body.

Heartworms are the most worrisome and can be prevented with a chewable tablet as prescribed by your veterinarian. Heartworm leads to respiratory issues such as coughing, exercise intolerance, a weak pulse, and loss of appetite. Heartworm treatment is intense and can only be administered by a veterinarian in a controlled setting.

Symptoms of tapeworms, hookworms, and whipworms include diarrhea, weight loss, loss of appetite, vomiting, thinning coat, pot-bellied appearance, lethargy, excessive drinking, and blood in the stool. These worms can be treated with medication as prescribed by your veterinarian.

CHAPTER 14

Traveling With Your Maltese

"The Maltese is the most wonderful travel companion! Small and compact, they are delighted to have their own travel purse or carrier and would much rather travel with you than stay home alone. In fact, to the Maltese dog, wherever YOU are IS home."

BARBARA SHEWMAKE
Storybook Maltese

Traveling can be stressful, whether it's the long car rides, unexpected flight cancelations, or delays. Bringing your dog along as a travel companion can make traveling even more stressful. Thankfully, Maltese are great travel companions and are the perfect size to take on trips with you.

Flying

Rules vary from airline to airline, but Maltese are generally allowed to fly with you as long as you give the airline a heads-up and pay the additional pet fee. That said, flying with your Maltese can be pricey as some airlines charge as much as $125 for a one-way trip. Many airlines require 48-hour advanced notice at the minimum, which can be done by either calling the airline directly or by updating your itinerary online. Be sure to check with your airline when booking your trip to confirm. Also, be aware that some airlines do not let any pets travel in the cabin at all.

Each airport sets its own rules and regulations for pet travel, so make sure to check with both your departure and arrival airport to review the rules. Generally, most airports require pets to be within their carrier from the moment that you step into the airport until the moment that you leave. The only exception to this rule is for trained service animals, which may walk beside you.

Mobile and online check-in have benefited travelers as a huge time saver. Unfortunately, most airlines require a visit to the front desk in person before they issue you a boarding pass. An airline representative will verify whether or not your pet is fit to travel based on Federal Aviation Administration (FAA) regulations and their own rules. At this time, a representative will typically ask for payment, all applicable paperwork, and verify that your Maltese fits comfortably within its carrier.

It's crucial to make sure that your dog carrier is the appropriate size. The FAA requires your pet container to be small enough to fit

Mary, Queen of Scots, had a great love of dogs, specifically Maltese terriers. When she was widowed at the age of 18, Mary returned to Scotland from France with her favorite Maltese dogs from court. Throughout her life, Maltese dogs would serve as constant companions. When Mary was imprisoned at the end of her life, her only cohorts were her dogs. One of these dogs even accompanied her to the gallows at the time of her death.

underneath the seat without blocking any person's path to the main aisle of the airplane. Since the amount of space available underneath each seat varies from airplane to airplane, airlines set their own maximum dimensions for pet containers. Pets must also be able to comfortably stand up and turn around within their carrier. We recommend getting the largest carrier possible to maximize the amount of space available to your Maltese.

Once you have your boarding pass in hand, you will have to go through security. This part of travel is typically most stressful for me if I'm traveling alone. The pet carrier has to go through the imaging machine much like the rest of your personal belongings. Lucky for you, you don't have to wait in line to go through the full-body scanner. Instead, you'll hold your furry friend and pass through a metal detector. Once on the other side, TSA will swipe your hands using a tool that searches for explosive residue. TSA may search your Maltese as well with a pat-down.

Photo Courtesy of Martha Burns

Before you board the plane, the airline's gate attendant will once again verify that the container size is acceptable. I have found that the gate attendant is much more vigilant in confirming the container size than the front desk. In fact, I've been turned away at the gate before for having a carrier that is too large. An airline forced me into purchasing an overpriced pet container from them to travel. This reinforces the importance of double and triple-checking to make sure that your carrier is the correct size before even leaving for the airport!

The FAA has very specific rules once onboard the plane: the carrier must be stowed before the entry door to the airplane is closed in order for the airplane to leave the gate. The carrier must be stowed the entire time that the plane is moving on the airport surface, which includes takeoff and landing, and the passenger must follow flight attendant instructions regarding the proper stowing of the pet carrier.

In addition to the FAA rules, each airline may have additional policies to follow. One policy to be aware of is the limit of the number of pets in the cabin. The limit varies from airline to airline. Much like how an airplane can sell out of tickets for passengers, it can reach its limit on the number of pets in its cabin. This stresses the importance of contacting your airline as soon as possible to add your Maltese to your reservation.

Other additional policies may include the number of pets that accompany you onboard. Most commonly, only one pet is allowed to travel per passenger. Another requirement may be for your Maltese to be harmless, inoffensive, and odorless. Some airlines may have you sign a waiver verifying that your pet is nonaggressive. An airline may require you to produce a health certificate. A health certificate, otherwise known as a Certificate of Veterinary Inspection (CVI), can be obtained by taking your Maltese in for an exam. In most cases, a CVI expires after 30 days. Your pet may not be allowed to travel if it is infected with transmitted diseases or is not up to date with its vaccinations.

Long layovers and long flights can be troublesome for your little Maltese. It can be stressful and uncomfortable to sit in a small carrier all day on a plane. Below are some tips to make flying with your Maltese as comfortable as possible:

- **EMPTY BLADDER:** Let your Maltese outside multiple times before you arrive at the airport and once more when you arrive at the airport. Most airports have outdoor pet relief areas. To prevent any potty accidents, don't allow your dog to overindulge in food or water prior to a flight. That said, bring along a small water bottle to keep your pup hydrated.

- **CARRIER COMFORT:** Make your Maltese's pet carrier as comfortable as possible. Line the bottom of the carrier with their favorite blanket and add a favorite toy. Add as many familiar scents as possible to keep your Maltese at ease.
- **PET RELIEF AREAS:** Aside from outdoor pet relief areas, many airports have indoor pet relief areas to accommodate long layovers.
- **MEDICINE:** If your Maltese has traveling anxiety, then you may want to consult your veterinarian for anti-anxiety medicine. Follow the directions for administering the medicine as prescribed by your veterinarian.
- **TREATS:** Bringing treats along is a great way to keep your Maltese distracted if it starts getting anxious. If your dog starts barking or whining on the plane, then try distracting it with a handful of treats.

Driving

Driving with your Maltese is much easier and less stressful than flying. Maltese are small and barely take up any space, so you can easily pack your pup in a car and take him along on a road trip. That said, driving with your Maltese still requires preparation and planning.

Some states have gone as far as requiring pets to be harnessed or strapped in while in a car, much like their human counterparts have to buckle up. Pets are considered a dangerous distraction similar to texting, eating, and talking on the phone. Some states require pets to be in a kennel and strapped in. Others require them to be at least harnessed and buckled in. Many states have banned dogs from the front seat, truck bed, or from hanging their heads out of the window. Keeping your Maltese crated while traveling is safe as it prevents your pup from distracting the driver and protects them from any potential hazards such as airbags. Avoid the temptation to allow your Maltese to sit on anyone's lap at all costs!

Crates are a great way of keeping your Maltese safe and comfortable during the drive. Check out your local pet store for crates that are specifically designed for car travel that are capable of being buckled into a seat belt much like a toddler's car seat. Crates should be kept in the back seat, as airbags can damage them. Make sure that the crate is large enough so that your dog can comfortably stand up, turn around, and lie down. Crates are particularly handy if your Maltese has issues with car sickness. This way, any vomit or other accidents are contained within the carrier rather than all over your car.

Pet seat belts are another option for your Maltese, although these have not been proven effective in protecting pets during car accidents. Pet seat belts satisfy the requirement of having your dog restrained so that it isn't moving about the car during travel and causing distractions.

Dogs are notorious for sticking their heads out of the car window to enjoy the breeze and new scents. Unfortunately, this is dangerous for both you and your Maltese. Your Maltese could accidentally lean too far and fall out of the window or could even suddenly jump out. It could be hit by another car, mailbox, or tree branch while driving. It could even get hit in the eye with a bug or other projectile bouncing off the road.

Instead of letting your Maltese hang its head out of the window, just crack the windows slightly so that the breeze and scents can still enter the car. This will also help prevent your pup from overheating during the summer months. Be sure that the windows are locked, as sometimes a Maltese's small paws can open and close the car window by mistake.

Some Maltese suffer from motion sickness and get physically ill or nervous when riding in a car. Symptoms of motion sickness include excessive

Photo Courtesy of Mary Lennon

whining, panting, yawning, whining, drooling, and vomiting. The best way to prevent motion sickness or anxiety is to make your Maltese as comfortable as possible. Bring a familiar blanket along for the ride as well as familiar toys.

Over-the-counter medicine exists for dogs that suffer from motion sickness. Medications that are effective in humans like Benadryl and Dramamine are also effective in dogs if properly dosed. Discuss correct dosages with your veterinarian before administering any medications. Dramamine should be given with a small amount of food. If you know that your Maltese suffers from motion sickness, then preemptively give your dog a dose before you leave for your car trip.

Micah enjoys traveling by car and sleeps through most of our long drives. We stop once every four or so hours to let him go potty. You should stop for potty breaks as frequently as you let your dog outside at home normally.

Overnight travel

Lucky for you, pets have become more socially acceptable as travel companions over the years. This includes overnight stays at places like bed and breakfasts, resorts, rentals, and hotels. It's important to plan your overnight stays out well in advance of your trip to make sure that there are accommodations available in your area.

Pet-friendly hotel chains include Motel 6, Best Western, Choice Hotels, DoubleTree by Hilton, Extended Stay America, Four Seasons, Hampton Inn, Kimpton Hotels, the Ritz-Carlton, and Westin. Another pet-friendly overnight option is renting through Airbnb. Be aware that these options, more often than not, come with an additional pet fee and possibly even a pet-cleaning fee. If your Maltese has an accident within the hotel or rental, then you may be susceptible to a high cleaning fee.

Contact your overnight destination of choice well in advance and inquire about amenities and requirements for your Maltese. Many hotels have rules about odor and behavior much like airlines do. A vocal Maltese that has issues with barking should not stay at a hotel, and you should find a more remote Airbnb or rental property instead. Some hotels go above and beyond by providing your dog with an amenity bag which contains treats, waste bags, and water.

Be sure to bring along a food and water dish for your Maltese. A leash will also be required when in the lobby of a hotel. A favorite toy, a bone to chew on, or a familiar blanket to lie on will all help make your Maltese comfortable in its new environment for the night.

Photo Courtesy of Irina Korovyakovskaya

Kenneling vs. a dog sitter

Leaving your furry friend at home may be the best option for you, depending on your travel plans. If you're unable to have a familiar family member or friend look out for your Maltese, then you'll have to hire a dog sitter or board your dog at a kennel. Each option has its pros and cons depending on your Maltese's personality.

The first option is the obvious one—try to find a familiar family member or friend to watch over your Maltese while you're gone. Your pup will be much more comfortable with someone that they know and will also be more inclined to listen to that person's commands. It's an added bonus if the family member or friend can stay overnight at your residence or at least have access to it while your Maltese stays at home. If your pup is headed to their house for a sleepover, then try to visit beforehand to make sure that it is suitable and to help familiarize your Maltese.

The second option is to hire a dog sitter—this can be either a professional or as simple as a neighbor. Maltese are generally docile and easy to care for. They are rarely intimidating or aggressive, which means that the teenage neighbor is a viable option for a dog sitter if you offer up cash. Just make sure that the dog sitter is qualified and that expectations are made crystal clear. A qualified sitter would be someone who has experience caring for an animal of their own.

You could also hire a professional. Apps like Rover and Wag! offer dog-sitting services. There are other online options like Care.com as well. Any of these options allow you to analyze potential sitters' profiles and make an informed decision based on their experience and reviews. You can find professional dog sitters for as cheap as $25 per night, depending on your area!

Regardless of whether you choose to use a professional or a neighbor, it's important to clearly communicate your Maltese's needs and habits to the sitter. Carefully explain your pup's bathroom habits, eating habits, and sleeping habits. Make your sitter aware of any quirks that your dog may have, such as aggression toward other dogs or even fearing thunder. Does your Maltese pull during walks and bark at other dogs? Are there any commands that your sitter needs to know? These are all important things to communicate!

The third option is to board your dog at a kennel. If your Maltese is timid and antisocial like Micah, then it may not enjoy this option at all. If your Maltese is social and enjoys being around other dogs, then it may love being at a kennel. Before you board your dog at a kennel, make sure that you read online reviews and visit the kennel yourself to see if the conditions are up to your liking. Most kennels require vaccination records and even health certificates. It's a big red flag if your kennel of choice does not ask for these documents.

It's advised that you search for a kennel that gives your dog playtime. This is often an extra charge on top of the kenneling fee but is well worth it for your Maltese's mental and physical health. Playtime options often include one-on-one handling and group playtime. If your dog doesn't get along well with others, then you should opt for the one-on-one sessions instead.

Kenneling comes with its risks—diseases such as kennel cough, canine distemper, parvo, and others are possible. Other risks include aggressive behavior from other dogs during group playtime. The good news is that most reputable kennels take hygiene very seriously and closely monitor interactions during playtime. Closely monitor your Maltese once you return for signs of disease, which often include coughing, lethargy, loss of appetite, or vomiting.

CHAPTER 15

Old Age

A dog's life span is unfortunately much shorter than a human's. Thankfully, many small dog breeds live longer than their large-breed counterparts. Maltese live 12 years on average, while the oldest living Maltese on record lived up until the ripe age of 20. That said, your little Maltese puppy will grow old well before you do. As your Maltese grows older, it's important to adjust its diet and lifestyle to make it as comfortable and healthy for as long as possible.

Eldercare for Your Maltese

Maltese are considered seniors at the age of eight or nine. There are certain changes that you need to be aware of and prepare for as your Maltese grows old:

- Decreasing hearing
- Decreasing vision
- Lower energy
- Intolerance for previously enjoyed activities
- Increasing sleep
- Drying skin and coat
- Decreasing appetite

You may have to rearrange your house to accommodate your senior Maltese. For seniors that have trouble seeing, you may need to rearrange furniture to simplify the layout of your home. For seniors with hip issues, you may need to get a stepping stool to help the dog up on a couch that they could once jump on to.

It's important to keep your elder Maltese active with walks and playtime. This will help keep your Maltese's muscles strong to prevent deterioration, move the joints, and combat stiffness. Be sure to play games like tug-of-war with plush toys that won't accidentally yank out one of your dog's teeth.

Be prepared for potty accidents as your Maltese may lose its ability to hold in its urine for long periods of time. You will have to let your Maltese outside more frequently for bathroom breaks and be understanding if it has an accident. If you are struggling with your senior Maltese going potty in the

house, consider buying potty pads or diapers. Dog diapers are effective in soaking up urine but are not effective for feces.

It's important to take your senior dog in for geriatric wellness checks. A veterinarian should be looking for things like cataracts, tumors, and other signs of illnesses that Maltese are prone to. Checkups should include a blood test, urinalysis, thyroid screening, and stool testing.

Diet for your elder Maltese

As your Maltese grows older, its appetite will continue to decline. A lower calorie intake corresponds directly to a decrease in overall activity. This means that every bite of food matters and must be packed full of key nutrients that will help your Maltese live a long and happy life. You should look for a senior dog food formula and pay close attention to your Maltese's eating habits.

A decrease in overall activity level is linked to mobility and joint problems. Maltese aren't as susceptible to joint issues as larger breeds, but these issues are still something to keep a close eye on. Look for senior dog formulas and dietary supplements that contain glucosamine and chondroitin sulfate. Omega-3 fish oils will not only help your dog's joints, but they will also help combat skin and coat issues as well as assist with keeping your pup's brain and heart healthy.

As dogs age, their digestive efficiency begins to decline. This means that food isn't digested as well, which results in fewer nutrients being absorbed into the body. Many senior dog food recipes contain a high-quality digestive enzyme that helps the dog absorb these essential nutrients. There are many over-the-counter supplements that contain digestive enzymes made specifically for elder dogs.

Elder dogs often suffer from intestinal issues in addition to digestive issues. If you notice that your elder Maltese's stool is abnormally loose, then you may need to switch to an elder dog formula with more fiber. If your dog is constipated, then you will need to cut back on the fiber.

Your Maltese's food also needs to be chewable. Like humans, many elder dogs suffer from dental issues, especially if they haven't had a good oral care regime throughout their life. Even with a good oral care regime, your dog's teeth will decline over time, and some may even fall out or need to be extracted. Try soaking your dog's kibble in a small amount of water to soften it up to make it more chewable. Other options include switching to canned dog food purees, which require next to no chewing at all.

Be mindful that poor eating habits may indicate underlying health issues. A sudden loss of appetite, nausea, and excess water intake could be signs of diabetes, kidney disease, or even cancer. Visit your vet immediately if you notice any of these habits. If an underlying disease has been ruled out, and your Maltese is still being a picky eater, then try mixing in chicken broth or warm meat to make the food more appetizing for your senior dog.

Exercising your senior dog

Keeping your senior Maltese active is crucial in preventing weight gain. Overweight dogs are at a much greater risk of developing disease. Older dogs also struggle to lose weight as effectively as younger dogs because of their mobility issues and slow-moving metabolism. It's best to keep your Maltese active throughout its entire life to prevent any weight issues.

You'll need to tailor your senior's exercise to fit its needs. For example, your Maltese may still be a puppy at heart, but it's important to not let your pup overexert itself. Elder dog's muscles don't recover as quickly, which could lead to injury if you don't allow your furry friend enough time to recover. Pay close attention on walks or during playtime for signs that your Maltese is getting tired. This includes heavy breathing, excessive panting, and slowing down. It's best to shorten up your walk and stick to play sessions in short intervals.

It's important to keep your Maltese's mind stimulated too. Try engaging your pup with brain games on rest days. Some brain games include hide-and-seek with healthy treats, dog puzzles, and doing tricks that your Maltese learned over the years.

As Micah ages, I fully recognize that I won't be able to take him on laborious hikes anymore. His joints won't be able to handle jumping up and down rocks and other obstacles on the hiking trail. Instead, I'll have to switch to flatter and easier hikes with fewer obstacles and less elevation gain. Elder dogs shouldn't participate in the same high-impact activities that they did as young pups.

FUN FACT
Marilyn the Maltese

American actress and model Anna Nicole Smith owned several dogs during her life, one of which was a white Maltese named Marilyn. The Maltese accompanied Smith to a number of award shows and photoshoots. After Anna Nicole Smith's death, her boyfriend Howard Stern took custody of Marilyn. Of the dogs, Stern said: "I love these dogs. They have helped me more than I've helped them. They were my constant companions after Anna's death, and were by my side the whole time. They were probably my only source of joy."

A low-impact exercise activity that is great for the joints is swimming. Swimming is a full-body workout that is used effectively in physical therapy for injured dogs. It's a good idea to equip your pup with a life vest. A life vest will help keep your Maltese safely afloat and your mind at ease.

Let's face it—elder dogs tend to be grumpier. A young pup that once loved the dog park may no longer have the patience to tolerate the chaos. Keep a close eye on your elder Maltese at the dog park and keep it away from dogs that are overly hyper. If you notice that your Maltese is growling or loses its temper at another parkgoer, then the dog park may no longer be the best place to exercise.

A little-known fact is that senior dogs are more sensitive to hot and cold weather than younger dogs, so be mindful of the weather. During the summer months, it's best to take your Maltese outside to play in the mornings or on walks in the evenings when it's cooler. Also, be sure to have a bowl of water available to help keep your pup hydrated. During the colder months, you may have to dress your Maltese in a sweater to keep it warm.

Saying goodbye

The hardest part for any dog owner is knowing when it is time to say goodbye to their beloved Maltese. Your Maltese's quality of life should be the deciding factor in whether or not it is time to say goodbye. Keeping a close eye on your beloved Maltese's quality of life is crucial as diseases and illnesses set in.

To put it simply, it may be time to put your pup down if it is having more bad days than good days. Good days include a wagging tail, perhaps some playtime, and eating and drinking properly. Bad days are measured by excessive vomiting, diarrhea, falling down, and seizures. When bad days outnumber the good days, it's a good indicator that your Maltese's quality of life is compromised, and it's time to say goodbye.

Other factors include pain and discomfort—if you are able to manage discomfort in your dog with either pain medicine or anti-inflammatory medicine, then your pup can still live a happy life. Issues such as labored breathing are signs that your dog may be in pain. A dog that whimpers at the touch or can no longer be held without yipping may be in a substantial amount of pain that warrants euthanasia. You don't want your Maltese to endlessly suffer during its remaining days.

Hydration is another key factor. If your Maltese is suffering from kidney disease and isn't getting its fluids through drinking, then are you willing to administer subcutaneous fluids with a needle if need be? You can quickly tell if your dog is dehydrated by lightly pinching the skin. If the skin slowly retracts rather than snapping back into place, then it may be time to administer subcutaneous fluids. If you're unable, then you may want to consider saying goodbye.

Mobility issues often lead to a poor quality of life for elder dogs. Can your Maltese move around the house without assistance? If not, then are

you able to commit the time to help move your dog around the house? Not being able to move can be mentally stressful for your pet. Immobilization can also lead to painful sores and the inability to scratch aging skin. Amputation of lame limbs is also a possibility. An animal that is mostly immobile but is still alert and responsive can lead a happy life, but if it is noticeably affecting your dog's happiness, then it may be time to say goodbye.

FUN FACT
A Maltese Writes Fiction

During the last two years of her life, Marilyn Monroe had a dog named Mafia Honey, or Maf for short. Maf was a Maltese, gifted to Monroe by Frank Sinatra. In 2010, author Andrew O'Hagan penned the novel *The Life and Opinions of Maf the Dog, and of His Friend Marilyn Monroe* which purports to chronicle Maf's life from the dog's perspective.

When it is time to say goodbye, you can either take your dog to the veterinarian to be put down or have a veterinarian come to your house to euthanize it. It's important to prepare yourself and your family mentally before this happens. Discuss this ahead of time with other family members and give them time to process it. Make your dog as comfortable as possible in its final days by taking it for walks, feeding it treats, and giving it a ton of attention. You want your Maltese's final days to be as filled with joy and happiness as possible.

You'll also want your dog as comfortable as possible when put to rest. Bring along your pup's favorite toy and blanket to keep your dog calm. The veterinarian will start an IV and administer a lethal medicine that is completely painless. Be aware that your dog may twitch or whimper during its final moments before it loses consciousness. The veterinarian will then leave the room to give you time to say your final goodbyes.

Once your Maltese is euthanized, you can either have your dog's body disposed of or cremated. Cremating the body will cost more, but you will get an urn with your loved one's ashes in return. You can either choose to bury the ashes, spread them in your Maltese's favorite outdoor location, or keep the urn displayed at your home.

Grieving your departed Maltese is a natural process. Everyone experiences loss differently— you may feel sadness or even anger. Seek out a mental health professional if grieving is taking a toll on you. The seven steps of grieving typically include shock and denial, pain and guilt, anger and bargaining, and depression. These lead to an upward turn of acceptance, reconstruction, and then hope.

APPENDIX

Resources for Maltese Owners and Prospective Maltese Owners

The American Kennel Club and the American Maltese Association are two trusted sources for information related to Maltese. They have in-depth care guides, services, and more to help you provide the highest quality of care for your Maltese as possible. WebMD is another high-quality source of unbiased information that will help diagnose medical issues and decide if it's time to visit a veterinarian or not.

American Kennel Club

The American Kennel Club is a registry of purebred dogs that is maintained with up-to-date and high-quality information about Maltese. It promotes events like the Westminster Kennel Club Dog Show, the National Dog Show, and more. It's the largest registry of purebred dogs in the United States and is the only nonprofit registry. The American Kennel Club is not only the most influential foundation in the purebred dog industry but is also the most trusted.

American Maltese Association

The American Maltese Association is the largest association in the world dedicated to spreading factual information about Maltese. In fact, the American Maltese Foundation helped ratify an updated standard for the breed in 1963. Today, the American Maltese Association consists of over 250 active members across the United States. They offer services such as dog breeder recommendations, rescue organizations, and more.

WebMD

WebMD is a fantastic source of unbiased information for everything health-related in humans, but did you know that they have a portion of their website dedicated to pet care as well? Be warned that WebMD should never be used to diagnose a pet's illness. The only person that can accurately diagnose an illness in your Maltese is a licensed veterinarian. With that being said, WebMD can be helpful as it relates to at-home remedies, identifying symptoms, symptom management, and more. It's a trustworthy website with articles posted and reviewed by licensed veterinarians throughout the world.

Made in the USA
Coppell, TX
09 September 2022